Benson of Cowley

Father Benson in 1903

Benson of Cowley

Edited by

MARTIN L. SMITH SSJE

Oxford New York Toronto Melbourne
OXFORD UNIVERSITY PRESS
1980

Oxford University Press, Walton Street, Oxford OX2 6DP

OXFORD   LONDON   GLASGOW
NEW YORK   TORONTO   MELBOURNE   WELLINGTON
KUALA LUMPUR   SINGAPORE   HONG KONG   TOKYO
DELHI   BOMBAY   CALCUTTA   MADRAS   KARACHI
NAIROBI   DAR ES SALAAM   CAPE TOWN

© *The Society of St. John the Evangelist 1980*

British Library Cataloguing in Publication Data

Benson of Cowley
  1: Benson, Richard Meux
  2. Society of St. John the Evangelist – Biography
  I. Smith, Martin L
  267'.24'30924   BX5199.B/   79-41264
  ISBN 0-19-213112-5

*Printed in Great Britain by Lowe & Brydone Printers Ltd,
Thetford, Norfolk.*

I

R. M. Benson:
The Man in his Time

A. M. Allchin

THE story of the Oxford Movement, and of what followed from it, is an episode in the history of nineteenth century England, which is at once well known and yet unknown. The sight of a group of able and enthusiastic young dons resolutely deciding to swim against the tide of their times was so surprising that the memory of it has still not altogether faded. To maintain that the Church of England was Catholic and not Protestant, that the only possible form of Christian religion was traditional and dogmatic, that the pursuit of holiness was the only satisfying end for man, was, to say the least, unexpected. Some memory of their exploit remains to this day.

One reason for this is the fact that the most brilliant member of the original group, John Henry Newman, was a writer of such distinction, and a personality of such fascination that his work has never ceased to attract attention in many different places. In the Roman Catholic Church in particular his influence has been and is immense, and at the present time it is probably growing. But leaving aside the case of Newman, it must be said that the memory which lingers of this movement has grown very dim. Neither of its other two leading figures, John Keble and Edward Bouverie Pusey, has received the attention which he deserves in this present century. Of what has been written about them, little has penetrated to the theological and spiritual core of their work, the real heart of their life and being. For here, in the reign of King William IV, was a group of men intoxicated with God. Any treatment which fails to recognize this fundamental fact about them, cannot hope to do justice either to their strangeness, their greatness, or their continuing importance for us.

The events of the first phase of the Oxford Movement took place within a strictly limited time, the years 1833 till 1845, and a no less strictly limited place. Oxford was still a world on its own. 'The scene of this new movement was as like as it could be in our modern world to a Greek *polis*, or an Italian self-centred city of the Middle Ages. Oxford stood by itself in its meadows by the rivers, having its relations with all England, but, like its sister at Cambridge, living a life of its own, unlike that of any other spot in England . . .' wrote R. W. Church in his classic account of the movement.[1] The railway did not arrive until 1844. The university was a little world stirring into new life after more than a century in which it had been distinguished neither for the depth of its learning nor the vitality of its teaching. Oxford at this time was still an Anglican preserve. Fellows of colleges had to be in holy orders and to remain unmarried as long as they retained their fellowships. Subscription to the Thirty-Nine Articles was required for entrance to the University. The 1830's were a decade of reform, and it became clear that the ancient and anomalous privileges of the universities would hardly be able to stand against the tide of liberal utilitarian measures. One of the reasons why the Tractarians caused such alarm was that it seemed for a moment as if they might, against all probability, succeed in giving new life to the University as a predominantly ecclesiastical and theological institution.

It was a small world in which people knew one another personally, a world of constant intrigue and faction, and of passionately held loyalties. Friendships acquired a particular intensity. Enmities were no less deeply felt. The leaders of the movement in 1833 were mostly young, in their early thirties, and many of them, like Newman and Hurrell Froude, men of sharp irony and wit as well as of seriousness of purpose. Between them they combined a number of excellencies, intellectual and spiritual, moral and aesthetic, which proved to be powerfully attractive. And all these gifts, this interplay of character and intelligence, of hopes and anxieties, was energized by one underlying purpose. For here were men whose lives can only make sense when they are read in terms of the religious dimension of human existence. In an age of prosperity and material progress, of industrial growth and imperial triumph, of intellectual ferment and growing scepticism, they turned their lives in a wholly different direction. They sought to bear witness to the transcendent reality of God, and to man's capacity to respond to and enter into that reality. The thirst for

Foreword

THE man in the street on being asked who Fr. Benson was would certainly have no answer ready. Even a student of nineteenth century Church history might well find it difficult to say more than 'He was a very austere man who founded an Anglican religious community for men known as the "Cowley Fathers".' Few indeed would be able to say more.

Except for a short biography written twenty six years ago, *Father Benson: Founder of the Cowley Fathers* by M. V. Woodgate, and two chapters in A. M. Allchin's *The Spirit and the Word* (Faith Press, 1963), a small book on nineteenth century theology, there has been little or no notice taken of one of the most outstanding English churchmen of the last century, whose life and teaching provide much to inspire us in this modern age.

As the present Superior General of the Society which Fr. Benson founded, I warmly welcome and commend this book of essays. It is something more than a collection of occasional articles. The contributors have been able to meet a number of times to discuss their work together, and though there has been no attempt to impose a uniformity of approach and outlook on their work, many of the essays have been rewritten or emended in the light of their discussions. They have made use not only of Fr. Benson's many published works, but also of the letters and papers in the possession of the Society. They have pursued the policy of quoting extensively from these sources since all his works are now out of print.

I hope and pray that this book will stimulate many readers to a fresh understanding and appreciation of the Catholic faith as it was lived and taught by this great apostle and prophet.

Oxford, March 1979   David Campbell SSJE

Contributors

The Revd Arthur Macdonald Allchin
Canon Residentiary of Canterbury

The Revd Christopher Rex Bryant
Priest of the Society of St. John the Evangelist

The Revd Mark Gibbard
Priest of the Society of St. John the Evangelist

The Ven. Robert Martin Colquhoun Jeffery
Archdeacon of Salop

Sister Rosemary Kemsley
Sisters of the Love of God

The Rt. Revd Lord Ramsey of Canterbury
Archbishop of Canterbury 1961–1974

The Revd Martin Lee Smith (editor)
Priest of the Society of St. John the Evangelist

Contents

To Gerald Carrington Triffitt
Superior General of the Society of
St. John the Evangelist 1964–1976

RICHARD MEUX BENSON: *Principal dates*

1824 6 July	birth
1842, 1843	travels in Germany and Italy
1844	enters Christ Church, Oxford
1846	elected Student of Christ Church
1849	ordained priest
1850	begins ministry in Cowley
1866	religious profession and foundation of SSJE
1870	Society's work begins in USA
1873	mission work begins in India
1883	mission work begins in S. Africa
1884	constitution of the SSJE framed and approved
1886	resigns from the pastoral charge of Cowley St. John
1890	resigns as Superior General
1892–9	resides in USA
1899	returns to Cowley
1915 14 January	death

transcendence which our civilization has tended to ignore or repress, but which now in the late twentieth century clamours to be re-accepted, filled their whole horizon. They were voices of its claim, men wounded with divine love, knowing themselves called to be saints. We are not surprised to learn that nineteenth century Christ Church, the most aristocratic of Oxford's colleges, should have produced nine prime ministers. It is more of a shock to know that it produced its visionaries and its saints. We might expect a French peasant who visited Ars in the lifetime of the legendary curé to say, 'I have seen God in a man'. We are less prepared to hear a Regius Professor preaching at the dedication of an Oxford College Chapel making much the same claim for the man to whose memory the college is built, but it was in no other terms that Pusey could make sense of the life of his friend John Keble.[2] It is in no other terms that we shall begin to understand R. M. Benson, the subject of this book of essays.

BENSON AND OXFORD

Born in 1824, the son of wealthy evangelical parents, Benson came up to Oxford in 1844, having already travelled widely in Germany and Italy. He was the youngest son and had been educated at home and by tutors. It may well be that his parents disliked the thought of sending him to a public school. The winter of 1843–4 he spent in Rome with an elder half-sister, months during which he came in touch with many prominent ecclesiastics, and was even received in audience by Pope Gregory XVI. He arrived in Oxford at the moment when the first brilliant phase of the Oxford Movement was coming to an end. The original band of friends was breaking up under the impact of Newman's impending conversion, which took place in October 1845. An undergraduate at Christ Church, Benson carne strongly under the influence of E. B. Pusey, the outstanding spokesman for the movement in Oxford now that Newman was no longer at its head. It is very typical of him that he should have chosen to identify himself with the cause at the moment of apparent débâcle. Signs of outward success were never of much importance to him. It is significant too that he should have felt the pull of Pusey's personality rather than that of Newman. A man of massive scholarship and complex character, Pusey had become Regius

3

Professor of Hebrew and Canon of Christ Church at the age of 28 in 1829. He was to hold these positions for fifty three years until his death in 1882. Pusey had been forced, by a series of personal losses, to go very deeply into the darker sides of Christian experience. His faith and prayer had been tempered in the fires of penitence and dread. His religion acquired a sombre tone, which was yet far from unrelieved. One of the most perceptive writers about the Oxford Movement, the Swedish scholar Yngve Brilioth, fifty years ago, described Pusey as the *doctor mysticus* of the movement. More recently Owen Chadwick has taken up this description, and remarked that whereas the word 'ecstatic' does not naturally suggest itself to us when we read the works of Keble and Newman, 'it springs naturally to the mind of one reading the sermons of Pusey'.[3] It is easy to be critical of the severity of Pusey's religion and of the increasing rigidity of his theological position. These qualities are perhaps best understood in the light of the gospel paradoxes that it is the meek, those who mourn, those who hunger and thirst after righteousness who are truly blessed. His religion, it is true, was not a comfortable one, but it had a transforming effect on many lives.

We shall find that the word 'ecstatic' is one which imposes itself on us more than once as we come to study the writings of R. M. Benson. They too refuse to fit into our normal categories, being at once mystical and theological, dogmatic and ecstatic. Moral seriousness is something which Pusey and Benson share with many of their nineteeth century contemporaries. The quality of their joy is another matter. From Pusey, then, Benson acquired many things which were to remain with him always and were to shape the future course of his life; not only, as Fr. Gibbard shows in his essay, a devotion to the Bible and a thorough knowledge of Hebrew but also a love for the Fathers of the Church and a firm attachment to the Church of England. Above all was the passion for holiness, for the experience of the knowledge and the love of God.

We must pause at this point to examine a little more of the convictions which formed the men of the Oxford Movement. For it is clear throughout that they regarded the doctrines which they held not as abstract speculations, but as regulative principles for life, social and personal. What they taught cannot be dissociated from what they were. As Louis Bouyer points out in his life of Newman, it is one of the greatest glories of the Oxford Movement to have held out a vision of Christian life in which the spiritual, the intellectual and the practical were so closely united. 'The greatness of the Tractarian movement is that it was neither a simply intellectual renewal, nor, like Methodism, a religious renewal without doctrinal basis. The theological effort brought with it ineluctably a spiritual revival, the most genuine religious needs were at the origin of its speculative research.'[4] The leaders of the movement were concerned to reaffirm the fullness both of Christian faith and life. They were seized by the vision of a Catholicism which was more than merely Latin, a Catholicism which would include East and West alike, and would replace the positive affirmations of the Reformers in the context where alone they make sense, the Church's tradition of sacramental faith and experience. They were renewing the original irenic purpose of the greatest of sixteenth century Anglican theologians, Richard Hooker. It is no accident that 1836, a crucial year in the early growth of the movement, saw the publication of John Keble's masterly edition of his works. Prayer for unity was fundamental to their understanding of the renewal of the Church. At the moment of Newman's conversion, it is typical that both Keble and Pusey should have responded not with polemic but with a call for increasing prayer for unity in holiness and truth.

Like Hooker, still more like Lancelot Andrewes, they were steeping themselves in the writings of the Fathers. It was there that they sought liberation from the shallowness of the popular religion of their days, as well as from the intellectual and controversial aridity of scholastic Calvinism and post-Tridentine Roman Catholicism. There they found a Catholicism at once personal and biblical, a religion centred on the doctrine of the Incarnation, and its immediate consequences in the reality of the sacraments as the way leading man to God. For from God's taking of our human nature there followed inescapably the call to man to enter upon the divine nature. 'Thus according to the Scriptures, the Sacramental Touch of the Church, is the Touch of Christ; and her system is "deifica disciplina", a rule which, in some sense, makes men gods, and the human, divine . . .' as John Keble wrote.[5] The doctrine of *theosis*, that God became man so that we might become god, returns to the centre of the Christian view of things. We shall be seeing later how deeply it entered into the thinking of and devotion of the subject of these essays.

Father Benson in the mid-1850s
Photograph by Lewis Carroll

THE FOUNDATION OF THE SOCIETY

How were the convictions acquired by Benson in his years as a student to work themselves out in practice? At first in remarkably unremarkable ways. Like so many others Benson took holy orders. After a brief period as curate of Surbiton, he became Vicar of Cowley, a village on the outskirts of Oxford in process of being joined to the city by rapidly spreading suburbs. In the 1850's and 1860's, we may see him as one of a group of young and active men in the diocese of Oxford who remained faithful to the original vision of the movement, and who sought to work out the implications of its teachings in pastoral practice. Amongst his friends there were men such as T. T. Carter, Rector of Clewer near Windsor, and W. J. Butler, Vicar of Wantage. Just as their diocesan, Samuel Wilberforce, was setting a new standard in the Church of England of a model, hard-working bishop, so they were engaged in establishing new standards of parochial activity. Both were men deeply involved in the renewal of spiritual life, directly associated with the first retreats to be held in the Church of England, and with the inauguration of parochial missions, founders of communities of Sisters, which by the end of the century had become large and flourishing institutions with branches in North America, as well as in India and Africa. These were all enterprises in which Benson too was involved. He became very much a part of the work of the diocese. So much so that when, after his mother's death in 1859, he proposed to go to India to found a missionary college and community there, the Bishop dissuaded him from moving, and insisted that he stay in Cowley. It was there at the end of 1866, that with two associates, one English and the other American, he laid the foundations of the first stable religious community for men to be established in the Church of England since the Reformation, the Society of St. John the Evangelist.[6]

From the very beginning the community brought together men of real ability. Of the original three, one, Charles Grafton, was a young American priest, a former Harvard scholar who was later to become Bishop of Fond du Lac. The other, Simeon Wilberforce O'Neill, had been a master at Eton. As his names suggest he came from an evangelical background, and like Benson himself combined much of what was best in the two great movements which had revitalized the English Church. In the

1860's he was working as Butler's curate at Wantage, and in 1864 and 65 published a series of articles on the missionary work of monks in the early centuries of the Church in the west, articles which ended in a plea for the revival of some form of apostolic monasticism. 1865 saw a number of meetings in Oxford and London to discuss the possibility of such a new beginning. It at once became clear that Benson should be the leader. Veteran figures in the movement, like Dr Pusey, were consulted; Alexander Penrose Forbes, Bishop of Brechin in Scotland and the only bishop at this stage to be in complete sympathy with the movement, indicated his own desire to join the brotherhood. Two young laymen, George Lane Fox and Charles Wood, later Viscount Halifax, were also considering the possibility of entering its ranks. It was a time of much expectation.

In the end it was Benson, Grafton and O'Neill who persevered. After a time of living together informally they took vows in one another's presence on December 27th, the feast of St. John the Evangelist, 1866, in the following form,

I, Richard Meux Benson, promise and vow to Almighty God, the Father, the Son and the Holy Ghost, before the whole company of heaven and before you, my Fathers, that I will live in celibacy, poverty and obedience as one of the Mission Priests of St. John the Evangelist unto my life's end. So help me God. Richard Meux Benson.

The others signed as witnesses and then made their profession in similar terms.

Thus the form of community life which had already been a reality amongst women for almost twenty years at places like Wantage and Clewer also began to grow amongst men. However simple the life at its beginning may have been, however many the outside commitments of the brethren were, there was no doubt in their own minds what they were doing. From the very first a full round of monastic worship was established, including the daily celebration of the Eucharist, the recitation of the seven-fold office, long times of private prayer and strict rules of silence in the house. But all this was done with the minimum of outward show. Benson was at all costs anxious to avoid the kind of romantic fantasies of monastic life which pursued other attempts at revival at this time. In these very years, a young deacon, Joseph Leycester Lyne ('Fr. Ignatius'), was involved in a number of flamboyant and

much publicized efforts to create a Benedictine monastery. There
was to be no publicity at Cowley, and the proximity of parish
work, with plenty of ordinary, routine tasks, visiting the old and
the sick, running clubs for the young and the children, was an
effective antidote to any temptation to medieval day-dreaming.
Benson was at this time closely associated with the first generation of Anglo-Catholic priests whose work in the slums of
London was revolutionizing Anglican ideas of parochial
ministry. Preaching about their work many years later he declared
that, though not under vows, 'they were living in all the rigours
of the Religious Life . . . their great leader [C. F. Lowder] was
wholly dedicated to God.' Clearly he felt very close to them. He
himself when he became Vicar of Cowley had lived at first in a
house of utmost simplicity in the old village street, a house little
bigger than a labourer's cottage. So now when others joined him
Benson remained outwardly the hard-working conscientious
Vicar of Cowley. If the casual observer thought that all that was
happening was that Mr Benson had a number of clergymen living
with him who were specializing in the work of parochial missions
and retreats, so much the better. There was no need to antagonize
people unnecessarily. Inwardly, as the essays in this book will
show, the reality was very different, but perhaps the depth and
intensity of spiritual life which was being lived in the nascent
community was in some measure due to the apparent ordinari-
ness, the down-to-earth quality of its outward appearance.

This concern to be adapted to the circumstances of the time had
one other consequence of vital importance for the Society itself
and for all subsequent religious communities of men in the
Church of England. The Society began with the approval and the
blessing of the Bishop, Samuel Wilberforce, and it continued to
work in complete harmony with his successors. It was fully and
regularly integrated into the life of the Church. There was no hint
of that secret, quasi-sectarian note which marked a number of
nineteenth century Anglo-Catholic ventures. Undoubtedly at this
point the personal trust and confidence which had grown up
between Benson and his bishop was of crucial significance.
Wilberforce had indeed sanctioned and encouraged the growing
sisterhoods in his diocese; he was at the time almost the only
bishop to do so. But in every case he had insisted that there should
be no vows. Now on this vital question he made way in face of the

9

quiet, respectful determination of the man who had suddenly become a 'father founder'.

The first two decades of the Society's existence show us Benson at the height of his powers and give us some idea of his extraordinary capacities for life and work. The work of a steadily growing parish went on; the Vicar interested himself in all its multifarious activities, from day schools and crèches to fêtes and horticultural shows. At the very same time he was expounding a monastic theology of extraordinary power and originality to his brethren, and himself giving the lead in all the exercises of community life. It is a striking example of the way in which in some individuals great powers of inward development are combined with equally remarkable capacities of action in the world around. Gradually more men came to join him, some of them also people of remarkable calibre. In 1868 it was Oliver Prescott, another American, senior to Grafton and a man of great ability. In the early 1870's came George Congreve, the outstanding writer of the first generation of the community, and Bernard Maturin, a notable preacher, who later became a Roman Catholic.

The numbers grew slowly but never in a spectacular way. Very soon however this little group of men living in a back street in Cowley had established houses in America and India and then South Africa. Benson himself went to make the first foundation in America, in Boston in 1870, and soon handed over the work to the Americans, Grafton and Prescott. In India it was Father Page and Father O'Neill who went out as pioneers in 1874. All these ventures were followed closely by the Father Superior, who seems to have felt himself directly involved in all the undertakings of the Society. He was an indefatigable letter writer, and kept in touch with the brethren wherever they might be. In the case of Fr. O'Neill, this habit gives us one of the most valuable series of all his letters. From 1875 until his death in 1882 O'Neill lived by himself in Indore, in conditions of the utmost simplicity. 'At nights he used to retire into the chapel upstairs and sleep behind the altar, where there was just room enough to spread his *shatranji* (carpet) on the floor and lie down.'[7] In the day time he kept open house in his little dwelling in the Indian part of the city, meeting all enquirers and working on a translation of the Psalms. During these years he incarnated that ideal of proclamation by presence and identification which has since been so widely acknowledged as amongst the most lasting and effective forms of Christian mission. As the size of the Society grew and its work extended—the South African mission began in 1883—so it became clear that it could no longer depend on the inspiration and activity of one man. By 1884 its rule and statutes had been worked out, and in the September of that year they were formally approved by Wilberforce's successor, John Fielder Mackarness. The bishop accepted the position of Visitor; the existence of the Society was officially acknowledged.

Two years later in 1886 Benson finally resigned from the parish which he had served so long. Four years after this he also resigned the Superiorship of the Society which he had founded. This resignation marked the end of an era, and was evidently not without tensions. The founder seems to have had problems in administering the Society, and difficulties in delegating his authority. For his own part he seems to have felt that the Society was becoming too much an institution. But whatever difficulties there may have been, there was nothing approaching a split. At the end of 1890, Benson left on a long visit to India and the Far East, arriving in Boston by way of Canada in February 1892, where he was to stay until 1899. Finally he came back to Cowley at the beginning of the new century, for a long old age, dying early in 1915 in the first year of the First World War. These latter years were as full as ever of many and varied activities—pastoral work, preaching, retreats, writing and publishing. Benson had all the Victorian capacity for getting an immense amount of work done in a limited space of time. But behind all the spread of activity there lay always another and more fundamental aspect of his character. In and through the journeys to different continents another and less evident journey was being pursued. One of the closest of his early disciples, Fr. George Congreve declares,

The consecrated man has not fewer interests in life than another; he may have more, but how many so ever they are, they do not divide, distract, exhaust him, because he holds them all together, along with himself, by a vital link to God.[8]

It was eminently true of Benson himself. It was impossible for his contemporaries to speak about him, without speaking of him in relation to God.

MEMORIES AND IMPRESSIONS

Let us then turn to them and seek to gather some impression of the way in which Benson was seen by those who knew him personally. We shall begin with two witnesses who had known him only in his old age, but who had lived their life in the life and worship of the Society which he had founded. Here looking back a generation after his death are two men, themselves growing old, seeking to see what it was that had formed the centre of his life. The details of the picture may have grown dim in thirty years, but the outline is still there and seen more clearly perhaps after long years of loving meditation. Here is Father Pridham preaching in 1943 a sermon at the commemoration of the Father Founder; and he can only speak of the mystery of Christ,

The glory of the Sacred Humanity, united indissolubly to the Person of the Eternal Word, in Whom all the fullness of the Godhead dwells in bodily form. The glorious mystery of the victorious ascended and exalted Christ; Manhood in His Person at the right hand of God. God glorified in His beloved Son, and His eternal purpose accomplished; and the Sacred Humanity in the midst of the throne the instrument of all divine action upon the world, and the store-house of redemptive and sanctifying grace for all His members. This the Father Founder's dominant thought—the supreme object of his contemplation, and the formative principle of his life and work—the ascended Christ.

As C. C. J. Webb remarked, what characterizes the Oxford Movement is not so much devotion to the cross, though that certainly is not absent, as a renewed sense of participation in the life of the risen and ascended Christ in whom God and man are for ever at one.[9] 'The mystery of the Ascension . . .' Fr. Pridham goes on, 'became the central object of his contemplation and the formative principle of his character,' the point around which his life inward and outward was structured and organized. And beyond that drawing to the ascended Christ, there was a still more ultimate attraction, the total offering of himself to the mystery of God 'with its transcendent claim on all life and thought.'[10] It is, we may say, a somewhat static picture of a life which was full of energy and tension, but it has seized upon the essential.

The same point is made in different terms by Fr. Lucius Cary, in a sermon preached in the following year. In a similar way he points us to the very centre of the matter in directing our attention to the patristic doctrine of *theosis*, deification. The position of Fr. Benson, like that of all the Tractarians, he tells us, involved an appeal 'to those great days of the Church's story when her doctors shed the light of their divinely-given understanding and wisdom on her questionings; and when the noble army of martyrs gave their lives with fortitude in heroic witness to their faith in the eternal life that was theirs in Christ . . .' The style may be outmoded but the words are carefully chosen. The Fathers wrote and spoke under the guidance of the Spirit; we too must seek such a life-giving inspiration from on high if we are truly to live in their communion and fellowship. The heroism of the martyrs was a witness to the reality of an eternal life which already before death was theirs in Christ. We too must seek to enter into that life.

In that rich age which comprises the first six centuries of the life of the Christian Church, deep in the spiritual heart we find that which speaks of the vivid experience of God's presence, and of the heights to which the soul of man can rise through grace towards union with God by knowledge and by love. It is a union so complete, by virtue of the divine indwelling, granted according to our Lord's promise (John 14:23), as to merit the name of identification; a union in which God takes possession, and guides and governs the powers of the soul; a union of which St. Paul says 'He that is joined to the Lord is one spirit and, speaking of his own experience, 'Henceforth I live; yet not I, but Christ liveth in me; and the life which I now live in the flesh I live by the faith of the Son of God, Who loved me, and gave Himself for me.' (Gal. 2:20).

It was no part of our Father's life-work to produce systematic treatises on spiritual states, such as those which have appeared in abundance since his day. But to those who read his writings with spiritual intelligence it is plain that the experience of that with which they deal was copiously there. Those of us who lived with him could see it in his whole life and bearing. It was not only what he wrote or said, but what he was, that we reverenced and, but for love, might have feared.[11]

It is striking how careful the preacher is to avoid all the technical terms of Greek theology, *theosis*, deification etc., and to remain close to the language of the Bible. But the substance of what he is saying is none the less clear. To speak about Fr. Benson is to speak about God's revelation of himself in Christ. 'I have seen God in a man.'

If in these pictures drawn thirty years after the death of the Founder, there is a sense of achievement and repose, far other is the picture given us by Fr. Congreve in a sermon preached in

January 1915, one week after his death. Here all is movement and life.

As we listened year after year to his addresses to his community in our annual retreat of four weeks, as we tried to follow day after day the appeal of that 'high-calling' and of that upward gaze of a soul inwardly contemplating heaven, we felt that that high reaching up into the light above all clouds implied a very clean parting with everything else for God, and the leaving of all selfish considerations far below. We knew intuitively that that high calling which never wearied, and that upward gaze, were tokens of a life-surrender that was absolute and irrevocable, of a mind so firm, and a love so loyal, that he attained to be himself living there where he was always calling us to climb.

All who followed his missions and retreats . . . could feel that; but we who lived with him in the old Mission House had other proofs of it. We all had our daily Eucharist, the Divine Office, the daily time for mental prayer; good times each day when we might recover a glimpse of our ideal, and hear at least a faint note of our high calling, and might be encouraged to look up again, and start afresh in the light towards the light. But there was always among us one who was not content to catch a moment's glimpse of the Light which is the Life, but had left the darkness and all indecision behind for good, never to return to seek any earthly good that could take the place of God, or come in any degree between him and God. Day and night it was always the same; that movement towards God, the leaving behind of all that hindered that movement, was never relaxed. Christ was all to him, nothing besides could be worth troubling about for himself, for he had all things in Christ.[12]

Such was the man; and those who shared his life were moved to reverence, and but for love might have been moved to fear. One felt in his presence a physical nearness of the realities of another world. Writing at the same time another of the Fathers recalls an incident in 1870, when as an undergraduate he was attending a retreat at Cowley.

That was my first sight of him, and it has left behind, through all these years, an ineffaceable memory as of a man belonging to another world. The words of the blessing as he spoke them, the tone of the voice, the upward gaze of the eyes, all struck home to one's heart as the most intensely spiritual act one had ever witnessed. It was almost like a physical sensation of contact with the spiritual world.

And this was not just the momentary impression of an imaginative young man. It was to be confirmed in many years of daily contact.

Afterwards, when I used to make my confessions to him, it was the same. The words of counsel which he spoke, and the extempore prayer which he usually made before giving absolution, had the same mysterious power. One felt bathed in a supernatural peace, and quickened with a tingling consciousness of the reality and nearness of spiritual things. Later on, when in 1879 I became a postulant, and all through the years I lived under the same roof with him as a novice, and then as a professed Father, it was still the same. Every summer the Society went into Retreat for four consecutive weeks, during which the Father Superior gave us three meditations, or more often two meditations and a spiritual instruction, each day. He spoke from his stall in the bare and austere chapel at the top of the old Mission House, in the cold of winter (for we also had a week's Retreat at the beginning of each new year), or in the sometimes almost overpowering heat of the July sun as it smote all day long upon the slates of the roof, sitting perfectly still with only a frequent uplifting of his eyes as if he contemplated a vision, pouring forth for an hour thoughts and words which carried one away into the world of spiritual realities. It was unlike any other discourse one has ever heard, spontaneous, copious, though often with a certain hesitation as if he were seeking for the exact word or phrase to express his thought, at times brilliant, epigrammatic, imaginative, and poetical, but always above all things vibrating with an intensity of spiritual vitality and power. His books . . . give no adequate idea of the unique force and effect of the spoken word in these Retreats.[13]

It is certainly not by accident that we can form a more vivid and complete picture of Fr. Benson conducting a retreat in the rooftop chapel of the original Mission House, than we can of him in any other situation. It was here, more than anywhere else, with the possible exception of the confessional, that he was most fully able to impart to others something of the vision and the life which was his. Fr. Maturin adds confirmation and detail to the description we have already quoted.

He wore an old-fashioned neckcloth, which had the appearance of being worn for several days, stockingless feet, and his girdle very tightly drawn around his waist. He was giving an address in the little chapel at the top of the old Mission House . . . . The chapel, like the preacher, was stern, unadorned, and uncompromising—no adornment except a Byzantine mosaic of our Lord over the altar. It was the embodiment of the poverty and detachment which were the key-notes of his teaching.[14]

Up till the present we have been listening to close disciples, to those who could remember him either at the end of his life, or as he was at the height of his powers in the first decade of the Society's existence. But the impressions of a more detached observer are not so very dissimilar. In a letter to his sister, written in 1893, Edward Churton, Bishop of Nassau in the Bahamas, says,

For myself, I had always thought him nearly superhuman, and this opinion is confirmed now I have had him as a guest in the house. One keeps on wondering to one's self how such a mind as his can have been produced? Fancy an old man like that—he is nearly seventy—giving us, four times a day, those marvellous meditations, in which sublime thoughts succeed one to another without a moment's hesitation, expressed always with a perfect accuracy and dignity, and often with a great force of eloquence; and so far as I could see doing this without any previous preparation whatever. When he was not speaking to us in the Chapel, he was either busy writing with the Hebrew Psalms before him, preparing for a new book, or else seeing us one after another for spiritual advice. For the meditations he had no notes whatever, and seemed to depend on nothing but the inspiration of the moment. That is not all: he is, what I had not known before, a very agreeable talker, and after all the stupendous effort of last week, sat talking today for an hour or more in the drawing room to Kilby and another young layman, besides coming to the Ordination and preaching two sermons besides. He is a sort of second Moses, whose force never abates. And then the indescribable sweetness of his character, which is never interfered with by the little sarcasms in which he delights.[15]

The picture is substantially the same. There is the sense of a mind which is not the product of this world; there is the same powerful unhesitating utterance; there is the same apparent reliance on the inspiration of the moment, which covers a lifetime of prayerful thought and meditation; there is the same relentless use of time so that not a moment should be lost. To these are added a slightly sardonic sense of humour and perhaps less expectedly, a capacity to enter into the give and take of general conversation.

A CHILD'S EYE VIEW

Of course not all observers were so admiring or uncritical. It was often complained that his sermons were too long and too difficult for an ordinary congregation. In public preaching he does not seem to have had the same control of his voice and his gestures as he had in the more intimate atmosphere of a retreat. On the former point, Edward King remarked, 'We follow him with a telescope, and now and then catch sight of him soaring in the heavens.' On the latter point, someone who heard him as a child remembers, 'When preaching he used suddenly to raise his voice to a shout, which made my mother start and set us all laughing.'[16]

The recollections of this last writer—we do not know her name—are particularly precious. They give us a very different insight into his character, and do something to soften the impression of unmitigated seriousness and severity which we might gather from other observers. Fr. Benson was, she tells us, one of her father's oldest friends; between him and her mother there was 'a very strong and tender friendship'. She and her brother seem as children to have been special favourites. 'My brother was known to him as "the little monk", and I at that age called myself the "'Dictine Nun", so that we always considered ourselves as under his special charge.' Immediately after his death she put down some memories of him, aware that she could bring out sides of his character which not many people had seen, could give us a picture of him, relaxed and at home in the family of an intimate friend. We are seeing the same person, but in a gentler and less demanding light. Even his sermons, though incomprehensible to a child and sometimes alarming, had their fascination for her.

I must very often have heard him preach . . . and though no doubt I chafed at the length of his sermons there was a wonderful fascination in watching his face, lit up by a light invisible and shining with radiance. I still have a very vivid memory of seeing him poised upon the chancel steps, for in those days we had no pulpit in our church and the steps of the chancel were very steep and high owing to the body of the church having been originally used for a school. He seemed to me half lifted up above the step, and when in later years I read of those strange levitations of saints I recognized how such things are but the outward manifestations of simple spiritual realities and perhaps the eyes of a child see things which are hidden to us later.

While the content of his sermons remained more or less impenetrable, there was something about the way in which he spoke and read, which even to a child seemed luminously clear.

Though I cannot remember his sermons—nor understood more than that he was trying to let us see that vision of the New Jerusalem of which he never tired to preach—I shall never forget his reading of the Bible. The most difficult passages seemed made clear as he read them to us. No commentary beyond his wonderful intonations and inflections seemed necessary.

This is not the only witness which we have to the very special quality of his reading of the Bible. He seemed to read it from within, so much had he made its contents his own. The words which the Spirit had given in the beginning, again in his mouth became spirit and truth. The tradition came to life.

Naturally enough the children were taught to regard him with a certain awe. This was, after all, a Victorian household. And they could see for themselves the truth of the stories they had heard about him.

Stories of great austerity fire the mind when young, and in the early morning when his door stood open, I looked in and saw the bed unslept upon and the floor strewn with torn up letters, and a pile neatly addressed on the hall table ready for the post . . . After a night spent in prayer and writing he would sometimes drop asleep during the day at unexpected moments. Once he fell asleep while hearing, I think, my father's confession and realizing in a moment what had happened, ejaculated 'Good gracious'. And often he dozed in the middle of an after-dinner talk, but waking up and taking up the thread of conversation again so that I think he was barely conscious he had slept. We used to sit motionless and trust that he would sleep for long.

Such a character might well have seemed frightening to a child. It is clear that many adults found him to be a most formidable person. But at least in this instance, this did not happen.

These things might awe one, but I cannot remember ever being frightened of him as a child, or ever trying to get out of his way. On the contrary I think he attracted children. His face used to light up with kindliness, and he would often tear off foreign stamps from the packets of letters of which his pockets seemed always crammed, and do little thoughtful things which win any heart but especially a child's.

Strange and awe-inspiring he might be, but he was evidently not devoid of humanity and humour.

He often fell into long fits of silence and abstraction, caught up to the world in which he really dwelt, yet coming down to earth again with a run. For no-one said more suddenly witty things than he, and bringing them out as he did with his hesitating nasal prelude they seemed the more forcible. He could also be most cleverly satirical . . . . but there was no malice in his satire, for he would always follow up a sharp saying by a laugh peculiarly his own and peculiarly catching. The merriment of the saints was certainly his.

Merriment is not a word which we usually associate with Fr. Benson.

There was something of the child about him which spoke immediately to children.

It was the human side which attracted me. The supernatural was far beyond me. But he was wonderfully human . . . Shabby, untidy, ill-kempt and quite eccentric, he seemed to the world an enigma and a puzzle, until now that he is dead, when indeed 'all men speak well of him,' but to the child through it all was a strange attraction. The other world which lies about us in our infancy lay around him always as a halo, and a divine tenderness shone through all that was most uncouth, and ousted shyness.

This childlike quality was with him to the end.

As he grew old and could see me no more, he said 'But it gives me great pleasure to feel your hand'. There could be no limitations to such a nature. If one sense was cut off he had the child's readiness to make up for it by something else.

It is a striking picture; the old man who retains the child's openness to new experience, the child's capacity to wonder and enjoy. It helps us to see more practically something of what is meant by a constant growth into eternal life.

THE HEAVENLY VISION

We have heard a variety of testimony to the impression which Fr. Benson made on those who came into contact with him. All have spoken of the way in which he conveyed a sense of the immediacy and nearness of God. There was something in him and around him which spoke of eternal and heavenly realities. Let us now for a moment hear some words from Benson himself. We know from what we have already read that the written word will not suffice to convey all that was imparted by his presence. Even so we can at times catch a glimpse of the glory of his utterance, particularly in the records of the retreats which he gave in the first years of the life of the community.

He is speaking here of the things which stood at the centre of his life; the nature of worship as realized in the life of the brotherhood, the present reality of the ascended Christ; and the way in which we are constantly called to go further into the knowledge and the love of God. He begins with a note of polemic, by no means untypical, against a backward looking devotion to the cross, considered as a moment in the past.

Oh! hear that voice, 'Look unto me, and be ye saved'. 'Look unto me'. Alas, how Satan would have us misread, misunderstand these words.

'Look to me not as I am but as I was' . . . 'Look to me upon Calvary and forget me upon the throne of my glory' . . . 'Look to me and be content to remain far away.' But no, 'Look to me' must ever mean, 'Look to me and behold me as I am'.

'I saw heaven opened and Jesus standing at the right hand of God'. Alas, that we should ever pray without seeking to realise the fullness of that martyr's vision . . . It is a vision which must move our hearts, which must unsettle us from earth, which must bear us onward to Him whom we love. Oh, glorious vision of the most high God! Glorious vision of Jesus Christ! 'Look unto me'. It is but the same command in other words when He says 'Come'. 'Come'. Yes. 'Come nearer'. Thou canst not look unless thou wilt come. Thou canst not come unless thou art careful to look. Look to none other. Look to me. Come onward to me. Come on through all those various stages of approach which I have appointed for thee. Come on through all the various ordinances which I have set before thee as the staircase of the heavenly ascent, through every sacrament and ordinance of grace, through every opportunity of Divine fellowship, in holy obedience, through every act of discipline whereby thou wouldst take vengeance upon thy sin, through every holy aspiration, whereby thou wouldst seek for something which thou hast not yet received, by every holy confession of thy fault, by every holy acknowledgement of my glory, by every vow of dedication that thou wouldst lay at my feet, by every act whereby thou mayst make more sure of the covenant of life to which I call thee . . .

Every aspect of the community's life, all the detail of its rule and observance are to be seen in relation to this one end. All of the means of grace are ways by which we mount up, meeting places between man and God. And then there comes one of those moments when the eloquence condenses into memorable words of power.

The vision which dazzles those that are at a distance is the strength of those that are most near. As thou comest on, come on with all the fulness of the eagle's gaze.

So it is that God calls us near unto Himself by the Person of His Incarnate Word, throned in the glory of the everlasting light. He calls us near unto Himself. And we if we would worship Him must know Him thus truly as He is. Yes, dear Brothers, so should it be with us. Let us seek to realize the greatness of the worship which we are able to pay, which we can only pay in and through Jesus Christ.[17]

To enter into, to sustain, to realize this worship, is indeed the very purpose of the community's life. The first question which St. Benedict directs to be asked of one who comes to join the

monastic brotherhood is, 'Does he truly seek God?' So here the
purpose of the monk is to draw near, to see, to love, to hear the
one who calls him out of this world into himself. The great
themes of Bible and tradition, of the monastic life as a journey
through the wilderness into the promised land of the presence of
God, of the call of the Lover to the Beloved come rushing back.
And again it is in the details of every day that the glory is to be
realized. The steep narrow stairs leading up through the old
Mission House to the Chapel, are to be the way up to heaven. The
brethren are to hear the call 'Come, Come, Come' in the strokes of
the bell ringing out over Oxford, just as for centuries on Mount
Athos the monks have heard in the beating of the *simantron*, the
call of God, Adam, Adam, Adam. And they will find in all the
limitation and repetition of the worship of earth, the richness and
infinity of the worship of heaven.

We come apart from the world to worship God. The children of Israel
were called out of Egypt that they might go three days' journey into the
wilderness to worship God. We are called out of the world into the
wilderness of religion, in order that we may worship, in order that we
may see God. God has appeared to us, and God wants us to come apart
from the world in order that we may see Him. He desires to show Himself
to us. He desires to make us experience the delight of His fellowship. He
calls us apart for this express purpose . . . 'The Spirit and the Bride say,
Come'. The Bride on earth, the Spirit with all the fulness of the utterance
of God. We are called near to worship. The voice says 'Come up hither and
I will show thee things which must be hereafter.' Oh! whenever we come
upstairs to our chapel let us think that we are coming up in obedience to
that command. Let us expect to have the revelation of God. Let us
remember that we are not coming up merely because we like to come, but
because the voice has bidden us come. The bell as it tolls seems to speak
these words, 'Come up hither and I will show thee things which must be
hereafter.' Come up hither to say words which thou hast often said
before, but come up hither to see a sight which thou hast not yet seen.
Come up hither to do that which thou hast often done, but come up hither
that I may do for thee that which thou hast not yet known. Our acts
towards God are very limited, but God's revelation of Himself to the
faithful worshipper is inexhaustible.[18]

THE UNION OF LOVE AND KNOWLEDGE

This is indeed the energy of contemplation, as it was understood
in the first twelve centuries of the Church's life, a knowledge
which is inseparable from love, which grows through the com-

munion of heart and mind with God, and through the communication of the mysteries of eternity in and through the acts of time.
We see how directly true it is for Benson, as Vladimir Lossky
affirms it to be for the whole Eastern Orthodox tradition, that 'to
know God one must draw near to him. No one who does not
follow the path of union with God can be a theologian. The way of
the knowledge of God is necessarily the way of deification.' The
given structures of the Church's faith, far from being a fetter or a
burden, become the means of our liberation. To quote Lossky
again, 'To put it another way, we must live the dogma expressing
a revealed truth . . . in such a fashion that instead of assimilating
the mystery to our mode of understanding, we should, on the
contrary, look for a profound change, an inner transformation of
spirit, enabling us to experience it mystically.'[19] Unlike so many
of his nineteenth century contemporaries who had thought to
find freedom through rejecting what they had understood as the
doctrines of the Church, Benson had found a greater freedom in
discovering their true purpose and significance.

So, though a man whose life was certainly marked by the
limitations of his own time and place, Victorian Oxford, England
at the height of its imperial power, something was disclosed of
another order of reality. We find him strangely independent not
just of worldly considerations, but also of the ecclesiastical
fashions of his day. An anxious, controversial theology is not for
him, since truth is not something we possess and must obsess-
ively defend. It is something which possesses us and can sustain
us, alike in life and death. We have to learn to live in a communion of life with the whole of the tradition of this truth, not
simply to repeat the formulations of the past. 'Orthodox phrases
are defended, when the Orthodox meaning has been lost. And
then not unfrequently, the old words come to embody false teachings.'[20] A striking example of this truth can be seen in Benson's
penetrating criticism of the popular Tractarian presentation of the
doctrine of apostolic succession. This crucial point of teaching
was too often expounded at that time as the handing on through
time of a supernatural power delegated by an absent Christ to the
Church's ministry. For Benson on the other hand, it was to be
understood as the sacramental expression of the real presence of
Christ through the power of the Holy Spirit in the whole life of
his body the Church, the same Church now as it was in the

beginning. No less striking is the way in which he consistently rejected the growing tendency among Anglo-Catholics to adopt uncritically all the forms of doctrine and devotion springing from the Counter-Reformation, practices many of which the Roman Catholic Church is now itself laying on one side as if not actually erroneous, at least often unbalanced.

Thus we find in him a capacity to be prophetic which can be startling. His awareness of the imminent collapse of the old Christendom, his vision of the true nature of Christian missions, are further examples which come to mind. His whole theological position, rooted in tradition as it is, is none the less turned toward the future. In many of its features it anticipates the developments of the last forty years and this is undoubtedly one of the reasons for our feeling of its relevance. His vision of a Catholicism which owes more to the Bible and the experiential theology of the Fathers than to the scholastic systems of later centuries speaks directly to the aspirations of our own day, and has great importance for the recovery of unity. His sense of the doctrine of the Holy Trinity as the living focus of all Christian prayer and reflection is characteristic of some of the most powerful theologians of our time, Catholic and Protestant, as well as Orthodox.

At times he felt himself torn apart by the difficulty of communicating his inner vision. There seems an irony in the fact that he should have been going beyond a merely intellectual apprehension and presentation of the doctrines of Christianity at the very moment when so many people were abandoning them altogether. In his urgent rejection of the penal substitutionary theory of the atonement, in his insistence on the apophatic nature of all formulations about God, he seems at times to be coming curiously close to some of his agnostic contemporaries.

'We must meet the agnosticism of the present day, which rejoices in putting God aside,' he writes, 'with the true agnosticism which rejoices in adoring love.' The very fact that he could speak of a Christian 'agnosticism', at a time when the word had only recently entered religious controversy, is itself significant. Again he is not afraid to take up the formula of 'honest doubt' and use it for his own purposes, 'The truest faith springs out of really honest doubt . . . That is no honest faith which fancies that it sees and believes too soon . . . That is no honest doubt which repudiates the unseen because it loves it not.'[21] But whereas for most of the Victorians their dissatisfaction with the theology they had known led them away from all Christian affirmations, in the case of Benson it led him on into a rediscovery of the nature of theology itself, as the experienced knowledge and love of the God who is beyond all experience and knowledge, and yet gives himself to us to be known and loved, a knowing in unknowing. He lived much, his companions tell us, in the realm of eternity. Perhaps it is not surprising that he should be able to speak to us so clearly across the chasms of the nineteenth and twentieth centuries.

In understanding how this may be, there is another nineteenth century figure who, I believe, may be of particular assistance to us, Søren Kierkegaard. He is also one whose work only became widely known long after his death. In Kierkegaard we find convictions which remind us of the attitudes of the men of the Oxford Movement, but held and expressed with a self-awareness and a sense of irony which they could not equal. There is for instance their common denunciation of Christendom—when all are Christians none are; their common conviction that sacrifice and suffering are things so deeply rooted in the heart of Christian life, that any Christianity which has made comfortable terms with the world can hardly call itself Christian at all. The situation of the Church of England in the middle of the century 'with its "smug parsons", and pony carriages for their wives and daughters'[22] was not so different from that of the Church of Denmark. Bishop Martensen might be first cousin to Archbishop Tait.

But there is more to it than that. There is Kierkegaard's fascination with the idea of the monastery, as necessary to Christianity; with the place of 'the sanctified one', 'the corrective' within the body of the Church as expressing the necessary counterpoint between the way of negation and the way of affirmation. Had he lived, he tells us, at a time when it was clearly recognized that suffering was inescapably implied in Christianity, he might have discovered how much of self-torture there was in his own temperament and attitude. But living at a time in which Christianity had become synonymous with comfort and prosperity he felt it necessary to make his protest as strongly as he could. There is surely more than a little of this in Fr. Benson's way of teaching by exaggeration. Above all it is in his thought about man's position before God, that Kierkegaard has most to say to us on this subject. The Greek word for monk, *monachos*, means originally, one who is alone.

When one is able to endure the isolation in being a single individual . . . alone before the face of God— then the thing of loving God and being loved by God will appear to him so blessed that for sheer blessedness he must say: O my God, now I have but one wish, one prayer, one desire, one passion, that I may experience suffering, become hated, persecuted, mocked, spat upon, put to death. For if God's love for me were to be expressed in the fact that in a sensual sense I enjoyed good days, that I received this world's goods, if it were thus to be directly expressed— phew, phew, that would be disgusting to me. I should die for shame, I should loathe it like an unnatural lust, feel that it was as disgusting as fat fish with treacle.[23]

To stand alone before God, to know oneself loved by him, to be able to love him in return, that as Benson says 'Had been too great a delight even to think of, unless I had known it as a necessity.'[24] How can man in all his finitude respond to this infinity of love? How can he let any other object save this have a place in his heart and mind? Thus it is as Kierkegaard assures us, 'renunciation, yea, the delight in renunciation, is simply a lover's understanding with God. So far as I am concerned, truth obliges me to admit that it was God that gave me the hint. I had not dreamed of it, I had not even believed myself capable of it.'[25]

No, man does not begin to believe himself capable of those things which are spoken of in the New Testament; we all underrate ourselves, our capacity for entering into the things of God, for responding to the God, in whose image we are made. We opt for *bourgeois* comfort and mediocrity.

. . . How ironical that every man is designed to be an Atlas, capable of bearing the weight of the world, and then to see what we men are. . . . But when an individual, not a mere simple man, but one who possessing primitive originality stands alone with the New Testament in his hand, ready to risk all and to suffer all, and says: 'No my good world, I have no intention of taking you as you are; here are the instructions how you ought to be'— that is an event, an event which moves the universe, is alertly observed by it— it produces an intentional change in the world, which a European war can be said to do only in a *superficial* sense in so far as it changes the political map; no, it is a change in the world, so that existence from its depths becomes attentive, hosts of angels and legions of demons set themselves in motion.[26]

The man who lives in God, in whom God lives, introduces into our world another order of reality. The same thought occurred to

Fr. Benson as he stood before the place where his closest companion and disciple had spent the last seven years of his life.

When I was shown the hovel where O'Neill lived, and the oratory where he spent his hours of prayer, I could not help feeling that it was a more important place in the history of India than many a battlefield marked by crossed swords upon the map. [27]

Existence from its depths becomes attentive to such lives of prayer and faith. In this volume we encounter a man who bears the weight of a world upon his shoulders.

2

The Theological Vision of Father Benson

M. L. Smith SSJE

'A GREAT theologian'—the phrase suggests, if not the creator of a dogmatic system or the distinguished occupant of a chair of divinity, at least someone who intervened significantly in the theological debates of his day or wrote works which came to be prized as classics. Fr. Benson was none of these things and to appreciate the justice of the title Bishop Charles Gore gave him we need to remember that at first it did not have these academic and literary connotations. Originally the term suggested the mystic and visionary rather than the professor—the contemplative teacher who shares his own experimental knowledge of God. It was thus that the early Church gave the title of 'the Theologian' to St. John and that Evagrius of Pontus could write 'If you are a theologian you truly pray. If you truly pray you are a theologian'.[1]

In this chapter we shall try to outline the theological vision which sustained his life and ministry. He himself never considered committing it to writing in its wholeness nor do his writings bear any resemblance to the elements of a theological system. In approaching him we have to divest ourselves of a literary conception of the theologian's art. Just as he is always concerned with the living voice of God and never gets trapped in a biblicism which identifies the Word of God with a book, a text to be expounded, so we are to regard his writings not as treatises but as witnesses which with the many transcriptions of his spoken word enable us to relive the experience of hearing his voice. In many of the sources this immediacy of personal address is very striking. It was the task of ministering to his brethren and other correspondents scattered in different places which especially stimulated his theological creativity. Some of his most remarkable thought is found in the letters which survive from those he wrote night after night rapidly and unhesitatingly without, needless to say, the thought that any would read what he was writing except the individual he was addressing. Similarly in his teaching ministry the present moment was all. As far as any could tell he never composed his countless retreat addresses or used notes of any kind. We owe the records of these astonishingly profound and closely-woven spontaneous discourses to the practice of taking them down in shorthand as they came from him in a stream of inspiration from the inner resources stored up by his own meditation.

His written works are closely akin to these records. In retreat addresses the spoken words are provisional and self-effacing; they may die away, their task complete, when the listener is moved to engage personally in the contemplation of the truth which they have served to disclose. His books are for the most part series of stimuli to meditative prayer, mainly expositions of scripture especially in the form of the liturgical lections of the Church. The *Spiritual Readings* for Advent, Christmas and Epiphany, *The Final Passover*, his six-part commentary on the Passion and Paschal narratives, and his commentaries on the Psalms and Canticles are typical. (In basing everything he wrote on scripture and liturgy we see his identities as an Anglican spiritual writer and as a theologian in the monastic tradition exactly coinciding). Everyone who picks up these works discovers that it is impossible simply to read them through. They demand to be used as a means to a deep assimilation of the passages with which they are dealing. In some of them each section of a few pages concludes with a 'colloquy', and this is no mere pious convention or padding but a concrete expression of the impetus towards prayer of all his writing.

The form of his teaching corresponds precisely to its content, which is marked by the passionate conviction that theology and spirituality, orthodoxy and life, dogma and contemplation belong together in organic unity. This quality of his thought can be considered from two angles. On the one hand we are struck by the doctrinal nature of his moral and spiritual teaching. He knows nothing of any mystical wisdom or ascetical principles which are not derived directly from the fundamental doctrines of the Catholic faith of which the creeds are the core. In practical teaching about the spiritual life, about conversion and prayer, he presents the great dogmatic themes of scripture and tradition as the keys, the enabling truths which actually initiate into experience of the Triune God. 'Those truths which Divine revelation sets before us . . . are not abstract considerations but active energies with which we must cooperate.'[2] 'The contemplation of theological mysteries is the very foundation of that practical life of holiness whereby we are to appropriate the gift of Divine joy.'[3] On the other hand we could speak of his experiential and mystical understanding of theology. Theological truth cannot be grasped except in a life of self-abnegation and worship. It is lifeless and sterile once it is cut off from its roots in spiritual experience.

This conception of orthodoxy as a 'living organism of truth . . . a living power, whose mysterious depths must be learnt by the teaching of the Holy Ghost "who searcheth all things, even the deep things of God"'[4] makes him a theologian in the patristic tradition. As Bishop Gore said in his commemorative sermon,

He was very orthodox, and a great theologian, but he had a dread of abstract or intellectualized, or what one might call scholastic, theology. He felt profoundly that Christianity is a life, a life which embodies a doctrine, and that true theology is expressed in life, and he found this kind of spirit most conspicuously expressed, expressed in its most classical form, in the great Fathers of the Church.[5]

This patristic and monastic instinct caused him to view the drifting apart of theology and 'mysticism' or spirituality which marked the transition from the era of the Fathers and the undivided Church to that of medieval Christendom as a disaster with fateful consequences. He wrote to Fr. O'Neill in 1875:

I quite feel that the practical neglect of the doctrine of the Trinity has been the great cause of the decay of Christendom. The Church—the Sacraments—Hagiology, I had almost said Mythology—have filled the minds of devout people, partly for good partly for evil. 'Thyself unmoved, all motion's Source', this great mystery of the circulating life of the eternal Godhead, has been almost lost to sight, spoken of as a mystery, and not felt as a power or loved as a reality. Western Christendom shut up the teaching of the Trinity in Latin treatises for the clergy. The people could not love God when they only knew Him in phrases which were to them an unmeaning jargon.[6]

This disintegration meant not only the distortion of popular religion but the perversion of theology. Fr. Benson was far from blind to the greatness of St. Thomas Aquinas and other medieval doctors but his appreciation of them did not soften the severity of his judgement on the rise of scholasticism. As modern critics in the Orthodox Church have done he regarded the rationalism of scholastic method as a factor contributing to the rise of modern atheism and agnosticism. He felt that divine truth could only shrivel up and grow dim if handled with a methodology which implied that human logic was adequate to demonstrate and vindicate it. Speaking of St. Anselm and the rise of scholasticism he wrote in 1880, 'And now it is to the same source that we owe the rationalism and unbelief of our own day. The dangers of philosophy in matters that are supernatural is overwhelmingly great . . . The moment we externalize ourselves from Him to consider how His actions and requirements fit in with pre-conceived human notions of divine necessity, we lose all sight of what He really is.'[7]

Scholastic methods of dialectic undermine the self-demonstrative power of revelation. 'Controversy kills divine truth, extinguishes the light wherewith it shines, in order to be able to subject the dead material to the processes of its own logic.'[8] It is the matter of revelation in this state of deadness which excites the justified revulsion of modern man. Fr. Benson had a vivid sympathy for the disgust for dogma of Victorian agnostics.

Christian dogma is often spoken of as very dead and dry; and indeed as men are apt to fight for it, it is dead and dry, and being dead and dry it has lost its very Christianity. It remains a dogma of the faith, but no more like the original dogma of the faith than is the husk that lies on the ground identical with the fruit once found upon the tree.[9]

How much of the repulsiveness of controversial truth and of men's antagonism to the faith arises from the grotesqueness of fragmentary statements which want the clothing, the atmosphere, the elasticity, the emotions of the divine life.[10]

All this is no mere anti-intellectualism. It arises from Fr. Benson's sense of man's capacity for more than a merely intellectual apprehension of God. He is made to know God with 'an active, experimental knowledge' through union with him, by participation in the divine life. Commenting on the text 'In that day ye shall know that I am in my Father, and ye in me, and I in you' (John 14:20), he writes,

The knowledge which constitutes eternal life is not a projected knowledge as of an external thing, but an experimental knowledge. We do not merely know about the Divine Relationships. That is only the dead form of knowledge which the intellect is capable of receiving. In spiritual life we know these Relationships by substantial identification in the Spirit of love . . . . This day of illumination is an inherent participation of the Divine self-knowledge.[11]

What is in question is not the denial or suppression of the intellect. Rather it is a matter of man's fundamental capacity as made in the image of God to transcend the limitations of his nature. 'Our knowledge of the Divine Being is in proportion as we are taken out of our own intellect to live in that very substance of God wherein the Three Divine Persons live forever One. Our nature is capable of receiving certain floating impressions respecting the Being of God but we must rise out of that nature if we are to know God.'[12] This is one aspect of his 'ecstatic' and dynamic understanding of human being which underlies all his teaching; we constantly come across the concept in phrases like 'rising up', 'stepping forth' and 'breaking bonds'. A comment by Rowan Williams on the theology of Vladimir Lossky is illuminating here.

To say that God is known only in the ignorance attained on the far side of ecstasy is emphatically not, for Lossky, a speculation about the higher levels of mystical ascent peripheral to the central areas of theological discourse; it is the foundation of a whole dogmatic system. If man's last end is *theosis*, the perfection of communion with God, and this is only realized through the ecstatic self-transcendence of human persons, then the capacity for *ekstasis* must be written into the formulations of Christian anthropology as fundamentally and normatively important.[13]

In the light of Fr. Benson's dynamic concept of man's knowledge of God it is easy to understand why he is so critical of the conventional concept of faith in terms of assent to propositions. Apprehension of the divine mystery is 'not the mere knowledge of a completed statement, but the continuous apprehension of a continuous reality, a living receptivity corresponding with a living object of contemplation.'[14] Man's knowledge of God can never attain any static term. 'Man is called to a life of eternal energy in union with God by His Word, and that life of active union is a life of progressive experience. The beatific vision will not be a stationary contemplation of a fixed form . . . . Man is called to rejoice in God's truth as a continually progressive acquisition.'[15]

We can be helped to see why the doctrine of the Trinity is so central for Fr. Benson by considering another comment by Williams.

The Trinitarian dogma proposes a model of personal being which radically challenges the assumptions of the fallen human mind; thought itself must be turned upside down by grace if we are to grasp the mystery in any way. The dogma is a 'cross for human ways of thought' because it demands a belief that the abnegation of self and the absence of self-assertion, self-individualism are the fundamental notes of personal existence in God.[16]

In man's fallen condition of selfishness and isolation his religious instinct seeking an object of worship can only construct a grandiose reproduction of himself—'an idol of the human mind, a magnified man, a dead God',[17] a being infinite but solitary. Fr. Benson regarded the notion of a personal God without real relations as fundamentally incoherent, and the attempt to clothe this being with the moral attribute of love no more than a projection. 'A unipersonal idea of God is not an incomplete idea. It is a false idea.'[18] The authenticity of the Christian revelation of God lies in its vision of a God whose personality is inherently social. Personality lies in relationships and in the reciprocity and mutuality of Father, Son and Spirit originates the love which pours forth from God. 'We cannot know the love of God except as being the exercise of that personal relationship by which the Three Divine Persons are distinguished; and if we lose sight of the Personality—the Tri-Personal Being of God—we lose sight of the relative energy of God within Himself.'[19] It is this sense of the explosive vitality of the 'circulating Act of the Divine Life', the coinherence of the three divine Persons, which gives an electric quality to Fr. Benson's theology. His meditations on the being and love of God teem with expressions of process, movement, power and action. The word 'energy' occurs with special emphasis and frequency; 'the relative energy of God within Himself', the 'Infinite Abyss of glorious energy'. The entire economy of creation and salvation is the expression of this energy of self-giving.

THE TRIUNE GOD AS CREATOR

The ecstatic, self-transcending character of man is a reflection of God's nature by which, so to speak, he goes beyond himself.

Russian theologians have spoken in this connection of God 'transcending his transcendence' and this audacious idea is not far from Fr. Benson's understanding of God's creative impulse. The created universe testifies to the essentially self-giving character of God who could not but 'burst the bonds of His own existence', as he daringly put it, in order to bring it into being. This is how Fr. Benson expressed it in a retreat address of 1877.

The law of the Divine Nature, whereby it is eternally self-communicative, is the basis of that coming forth of power whereby God created the world. It was not a mere accident that God thought about creation. The calling of creation into existence was in some way a necessity of the procession of the Holy Ghost. As God is eternally self-communicative, the love of God eternally proceeding within the Godhead; so He invented this mystery of time, and having burst the bonds of His own Divine existence, He called into existence these subordinate agencies in which we have our part.[20]

This insight comes not through philosophical speculation but through experience of the Spirit. In the life of prayer and conversion comes a deep sense of the fragility of creaturely being, its precarious nothingness in inconceivable contrast to the being of God, and yet together with this comes the experience of his costly self-communication to us over this seemingly unbridgeable gulf. So Fr. Benson first coins this phrase which stands for the divine self-transcendence, 'bursting the bonds of the divine nature', when describing what is known in the spiritual life. 'The Holy Ghost seems, as it were, to burst the bonds of the divine nature, the bonds of infinity, in order to sanctify us fallen creatures.'[21]

Our sanctification is nothing less than our admission into the Divine Life, our deification, and Fr. Benson regards this as the clue to the very concept of creation itself. Creation implies the ultimate readiness on God's part to receive creatures into union with himself. However glorious the universe may be it is not worthy of God if it is to be left over against and outside himself 'to glitter as a toy in the Divine Presence'. 'The fitness of things necessitates the exaltation of the finite to partake of the glory of the infinite, if the work is to be worthy of God.'[22]

The power of God exerted in Creation would not have a result equal to the effort if it had demanded the Almighty power for its origin and had died out in the Creature. It is the eternally predestined glory of the Incarnation which (so to speak) saves the act of Creation from being unworthy of God. We cannot understand how Creation is to be perfected in God, but we can perceive that no object could be worthy of the Divine Majesty which did not attain to the perfection of God. Neither could any creature attain to that perfection without being made partaker of the Divine Nature.[23]

Fr. Benson's theological vision has a markedly different character from those based on the standard theory that the Incarnation was contingent on the Fall; to put it crudely, a divine afterthought for remedying the catastrophe of man's alienation from God. He committed himself in the original creative act to the Incarnation, by which the 'law of the Eternal Generation' was to be introduced into creation to transform it from within.

Fr. Benson could write eloquently about the glory of the universe as we contemplate it as an expression of the infinitely complex and rich life of the triune Creator, and about the importance for the Church of scientific endeavour as a means of revealing the splendours of the divine wisdom. But readers tend to be aware more of the forceful way he writes of nature's 'emptiness' and 'nothingness', expressions which have a jarring negativity to modern ears. Why he uses these terms so uncompromisingly is surely because he believed that the Incarnation which was predestined in the original creative impulse was the Incarnation as we witness it in the life, death and resurrection of Jesus, and that this must be decisive in the estimate we have of creation. If the Incarnation had been a triumphant theophany there would be no cause to speak of nature's nothingness. But the divine Word 'emptied himself, taking the form of a servant, being made in the likeness of men. And being found in fashion as a man, he humbled himself, becoming obedient even unto death, yea, the deaths of the cross' (Phil. 2:7,8). The cross reveals that our creaturely being is of itself 'being towards death', tending towards annihilation, for in assuming our nature the Son himself had indeed to be drawn into this death. Benson's uncompromising assertion of the emptiness of nature is the measure of the deep seriousness with which he took the revelation of God's *kenosis*, self-emptying, and it gives to his theology of hope a great sense of victory since through the Incarnation 'the creation itself also shall be delivered from the bondage of corruption into the liberty of the glory of the children of God' (Rom. 8:21).

Kenosis, then, is written into the very concept of creation in the sense that the creative energy itself is that of costly self-giving love. In Lossky's words 'God went out from himself, so to speak,

in order to create. There is a moment . . . of a certain humiliation, a self-emptying, which is greater than that theology which
always wants to be fixed on the majesty of God.'[24] It is a love
which is prepared for the ultimate cost of bringing creation to its
fulfilment by saving it from its nothingness from within. 'Creation involved the humiliation of Almighty God, even to the death
of the Cross so that it might at last be taken up into the glory of the
Uncreated Life.'[25]

MAN AND THE FALL

Fr. Benson handled the myth of the Fall with considerable freedom and obviously did not feel bound to one consistent interpretation. When the theme does occur it effectively illustrates some
of the emphases typical of him. The traditional theology of the
manuals which dwelt on the perfections of paradisal man is completely absent. He is much more in the tradition of Irenaeus and
thinks of human nature in terms of development and growth. In
paradise man was in a state of imperfection and potentiality in
which he had to be patient. 'Man was put in a condition of
progress to be gradually brought onward to that which was for the
time beyond his reach . . . Man then ought to have found his joy
in looking forward to that perfection which God would give him
eventually.'[26] This was no passive condition of patience but one
of conflict and vigilance, for Fr. Benson took very seriously the
myth of the angelic fall and regarded the creation of the earth as
taking place within the atmosphere, so to speak, of Satanic antagonism. This theme, that strife and spiritual conflict are basic to
the human condition, underlies his whole spirituality. The Fall
then consisted in yielding to the persuasion of Satan 'to seize
upon these higher gifts at once' by man's own initiative and
strength, rebelling against the necessity of receiving them as the
progressive gift of God. He saw the consequence of the Fall as the
forfeiture of life, the forfeiture of the Holy Spirit, rather than the
incurring of guilt, but what stimulated his most imaginative
writing was the theme of the forfeiture of human solidarity. Had
the image of God in man been unimpaired the human race would
have come to be a living reflection of the Trinity.

The collective whole of an unfallen humanity would have been a universe
of life in which all individuals would have had their part. The joy of each

would have been to live not only *for* all but to live *in* all. None could have had any separate individual interest any more than the eye or the hand or the foot have separate interests in the bodily organism . . . . The multiplicity in unity would have been the created manifestation of Divine Life. [27]

We can begin to understand why he emphasized the opposition of the Church and the world when we appreciate the contrast between the vision of the human race as called to be an organism of mutual service and vital interdependence, and society as he saw it riddled with the competitive values of laissez-faire capitalism. The ideals of socialism might seem to us to correspond much more closely to his own but he refused to believe that political measures were capable of healing the spiritual alienation of man which could only corrode from within all merely human structures designed to restore the organic unity of society. Insofar as socialism sought to achieve by autonomous human effort what could only be given by God it reproduced the very movement of rebellion which constituted the Fall.

This doctrine of the social nature of man means that the idea of the Church is implied in the very definition of man; the Church is the realization of his nature. 'We must not think of the Church as if it existed for our salvation. It would equally have existed had we never needed to be saved.'[28] Secondly the popular Protestantism which represented Christianity in terms of the salvation of individual souls was a terrible distortion of the gospel. Man can only be saved collectively in a social organism in which the relativity of his nature can come to realization. When it came to addressing the young Society of St. John the Evangelist on the question of community life as a specially intense realization of the common life of the Church in which man's true nature is restored, he expounded the theme with quite extraordinary power.

Thy whole life must be a *relative* life. The moment thou art imprisoned in thine own self-consciousness, in thine own separate individuality, in the selfishness of thine own separate existence, thou committest a worse suicide than taking the life of thy body. Thou destroyest the very life of thy person. Thy person is a relative being and thou hast no existence save when thou actest for others. Man is created to be a social being, as God is a social Being. And as the Three Divine Persons have no life whatsoever except in this relativity of action, so have we no life whatsoever except in relative action towards others . . . It is the law of our nature that our life is personal, relative, communicating all that it has. It is the law under which the Christian Church, the Body of Christ, is constituted. 'They had all things in common'. Property belongs to the dead world. Community is the life of God.[29]

THE INCARNATION AND THE HOLY SPIRIT

We are now in a position to realize how absolutely central to his theology the Incarnation is; incarnation which is not a mere 'transient theophany' or an expedient whereby in the past an atoning transaction was accomplished, but is a mystery, as he audaciously puts it, 'greater than that of Creation. It was a great act to call out of infinite nothingness, finite being. It is a greater act to call finite being into infinite glory . . . . So God sent His Son to take upon Himself created nature, that the Word being made flesh might raise created nature to the fellowship of the divine glory.'[30] This is of course a representation of the vision of the Greek Fathers. But as soon as we examine his teaching in detail we notice emphases peculiar to himself and one of the most significant of these is his stress on the procession of the Holy Spirit from the Father *and the Son* as vital to understanding the Incarnation; this is one of the points where he differs from the eastern theological tradition with which he has in many other respects more affinity than the western.

Fr. Benson was critical of the way in which the '*filioque*' clause had been expounded in the West and regarded the eastern Churches' retention of the older doctrine of the Procession from the Father as an important ecumenical witness; nevertheless he looked on the western addition to the creed as no mere peripheral speculation but as a vitally important theological key. What was for others merely part of the inherited stock in trade of the western tradition evoked in him an intense response. In this quotation from a retreat address he does less justice to the personality of the Spirit than in many other expositions of the theme, but the sense of movement and energy is very typical.

'As the Father hath life in Himself, so hath He given the Son to have life in Himself'. As the Father hath life which is energetic, so hath the Son life energetic; and so is the procession of the Holy Ghost the proceeding forth of the exhaustless energy of that undivided life. Not life, such as we call this life of ours, which is rather but an imprisoned capacity of life, — death (more truly than life). Not such is the life of the Father, not such is the life of the Son. There is no limitation to the proceeding forth of the fullness of the eternal will, the undivided energy not expending itself as it comes forth of its own eternal joy of exhaustless power. 'The Holy Ghost proceeding from the Father and the Son'. It is by one act of spiration, one act of Divine life. He is the Spirit of the Father, and the Spirit of the image of the Father.[31]

When the credal affirmation (so often left theologically unassimilated) that Christ was conceived by the Holy Spirit is read in the light of this doctrine it gives a new dimension to the doctrine of the Incarnation. In emptying himself the Son remains the one from whom the divine Spirit flows on. It is the Spirit proceeding from him who takes up and anoints and fills the humanity he assumes and it is by that Spirit that this new humanity is communicable, transmissible to men. 'In the Person of the Holy Ghost the Divine Nature returns as it were to its source by a circulating act of life. If the Divine Nature had come forth into our humanity without this reflexive principle, it would have gone forth to lose itself in creation instead of uplifting creation into God.'[32] This is how he understands the very name of Christ. 'The Holy Ghost anointed that manhood, springing up within it as the Divine grasp whereby the Son of God took it upon Himself so that no particle or element of the nature could be owned by the Son as belonging to His Body unless the Holy Ghost filled it with a supernatural Divine Life.'[33]

There is a flawed side to Fr. Benson's theology, a tendency to let the light of grace cast nature into too deep a shadow, and his stress on the Virgin Birth and the sheer passivity of Mary in the recreative miracle of the Incarnation led him to use harsh forms of expression which make too violent a discontinuity between the humanity of Adam and the new creation in her womb. On the other hand there is nothing frigid or static about his account of the Spirit-filled manhood of the mediator. The Incarnation is process: 'The Manhood thus was taken into God *as the human structure developed.*'[34] He protests against the representation of the humanity of Christ 'as the slavish instrument of a Divine Person' whereas it acts with a spontaneity, intelligence and love intensified by growing obedience and responsiveness to the anointing Spirit.

The central theme of the atoning, redemptive purpose of the Incarnation is fully expounded in the chapter by Bishop Michael

Ramsey but we can point out several associated themes. One is Fr. Benson's conviction that the Incarnation involved suffering whether there was an atonement to be wrought or not. Suffering was not an external penal imposition, as implied in the substitutionary theories of evangelicalism; not just the measure of Christ's complete obedience or a matter of his sin-bearing; but mysteriously an inevitable condition of divine existence in human form. 'God, in assuming our nature, chose to act under a form, which, in the very nature of things, involved suffering, for it was a limitation of the Divine glory, and therefore every faculty of the nature so assumed had to feel the strain of the supernatural.'[35] This gives a clue to the emphasis he places on suffering in man's spiritual life which is not a morbid dolourism. Our inner sufferings as Christians are closely related to the Lord's; it is our humanity being put under stress from within as it is expanded, stretched and made to grow by the divine life communicated to us. The Spirit 'accommodates Himself to our littleness that we may expand to His greatness; we must bear the pain of expansion . . . We are stretched indeed not on the rack of human torture, but on the glorious Being of the Holy Ghost.'[36]

Secondly, the suffering of the incarnate Lord stems from the completeness of his identification with mankind in their suffering and sin, in 'continuous sympathetic life' and in participating in man's vulnerability to Satan. Once again we see his grasp of the solidarity of mankind. 'The mystery of atonement brings before us the unity of the human race, the continuous vitality of mutual interest . . . . This law of loving sympathy is the basis of the atonement.'[37]

As for the victory over death in the deepest experience of this vulnerability, the dereliction of the cross, Fr. Benson underlines the reference in the Epistle to the Hebrews that it was by the eternal Spirit that Christ offered himself without spot to God. 'The Second Person of the Godhead acted in the weakness which belonged to our flesh by reason of the Fall; not with a charmed life of insensibility arising from Divine omnipotence but by the power of the Holy Ghost continually developed by the action of His Human Will'.[38] This is a theological theme with considerable bearing on the practice of the Christian life. The same victory is capable of being extended and continually reproduced in our own lives precisely because 'that same Spirit dwells as personally with each of the faithful members of Christ's Body as He dwelt with Christ the Head'.[39]

The unwavering consistency of his concern to interpret the role of the Holy Spirit throughout the entire economy of creation and recreation, this constant unfolding of the interdependence, mutual interaction and indissoluble unity of the divine persons is what makes his theology far more significant than merely an eloquent reworking of traditional themes. It means he is at his strongest where western theologians have usually been at their weakest.

THE RESURRECTION AND ASCENSION

We see this consistency maintained in his theology of the Resurrection. In expounding the fourth verse of the first chapter of the Epistle to the Romans, where Jesus is said to have been 'declared to be Son of God with power, according to the spirit of holiness, by the resurrection from the dead' he claims that here the resurrection does not refer merely to the resurrection of Christ himself. It is 'the raising up of others along with Himself as the first fruits from the dead—the communication of the Life of God by the power of the Spirit of Holiness to others—which shows that He is not merely the object *on* which the Holy Ghost works, but the Lord of Life and Glory, *from* whom the Holy Ghost proceeds to carry out the work of sanctification.'[40] In the Resurrection and Ascension the glorified Body of Christ, from being the limiting mode of his self-emptying, is transformed into a living organism into which the Spirit which fills it can absorb and implant those who believe, an organism in whose expansion and growth to final completeness the whole process of creation finds its consummation. We have already seen how strong Fr. Benson's sense of process was and he grasped the bearing the idea of development and evolution in post-Darwinian science had on the Christian doctrine of the final 'pleroma' of the risen Christ.

The previous stages of development by which some suppose that our body attained its present form may well (if admitted) be supposed to act as a prelude to this final transformation of man's body by the resurrection of Christ as a fresh germinal principle of life. The whole system of development gains indeed a purpose and a finality if it culminate in the exaltation of Christ to the throne of creation, whereas it is aimless if the highest result be nothing more than our present human form of life upon the earth.[41]

Later in speaking about the growth of the Church as Christ 'feeding upon the world, uniting it to Himself that He may sanctify it', he sets it in the context of the cosmic process. 'Thus He is forming that new heaven and earth wherein dwelleth righteousness. That final consummation whereby God shall become all in all is the final completion of a process of elevation and spiritual development operating in the created world from the beginning'.[42]

There are many themes woven together to form his visionary theology of the Ascension, the great focus of Fr. Benson's religion. He was fascinated by the interval between the Ascension and Pentecost as suggesting a process of intensifying glory and expanding sovereignty as Jesus passes through the ranks of the angelic hierarchy. His meditations constantly return to the theme of Jesus's personal human joy in his exaltation. 'His Humanity rejoices to be welcomed and rewarded as the Father's Son with the infinity of eternal love flowing forth in the perfected consciousness of His human nature, made perfect through suffering, gladdened for ever with the unction of Divine bliss, as He gazes upon Him whose Image He is.'[43] But he also characteristically underscores the corporate nature of the Ascension. As the Lord of Hosts, he does not ascend alone; his mystical body is already constituted by the 'saints' whose bodies rose with his own body as being his members and appeared to many (Matt. 27:52) and now share his Ascension. The theme finds its most remarkable expression when Fr. Benson discusses the idea that already in the last supper the body of Christ had 'extended itself', so to speak, in Christ's gift of himself to the Apostles in his body and blood. In a striking and original way he sees this as the key to the mystery of Pentecost: the flowing through the whole body of the anointing Spirit in consequence of the glorification of the head. This passage from a Whitsuntide letter of 1875 is one of the best remembered of his writings and the great Russian theologian Bulgakov once expressed a wish that he had written it himself.

So He passes on beyond them to take the glory of God at the right hand of God. But there He is not glorified in His own Person only. His Apostles had fed upon Him, had His Body within them by virtue of the Holy Eucharist, although they had not yet come to live thereby. He was in them, but they were not yet in Him. Now, upon His Ascension, His Body in them is glorified instantaneously with the glorifying of His body at the right hand of God. Like an electric flash the glory of the Spirit shines out in the fires of Pentecost. The body of Christ, however veiled in our flesh, in our sinful persons, nevertheless cannot but have the glory of the Spirit of holy fire burning and resting upon it. We do not, I think, dwell as we ought to dwell on the *present* glorification of our natures in our own persons, as the members of the glorified body of Christ. It is this which the Apostle presses as the argument against sin, 'He . . . that despiseth, despiseth not man, but God'—God present within himself; and it was this cherished remembrance which enabled the early Christians to triumph over the world.[44]

These last remarks are characteristic and important. His vision of glory is not one of those which is so sublime and uplifting that it cuts the nerve of conflict and struggle. It is the very thing that empowers us for the fight. The letter continues by warning about the converse phenomenon. Slackening of Christian resistance and non-conformity will be registered by a fading of the sense of identification with Christ and an urgent faith focused 'on the contemplation of Jesus at the right hand of God', and its replacement by backward-looking devotion centred on the historical consideration of the earthly life and Passion of Christ.

THE SACRAMENTS

We are now in a position to evaluate the tremendous weight Fr. Benson places on the sacraments. For all his deep awareness of the cosmic scope of the Incarnation he did not lose hold of the biblical idea of covenant with all its concreteness and particularity.

Christ took upon Himself our nature; but He did not sanctify mankind in its totality, although He sanctified our nature in its completeness . . . He called His disciples 'out of the world', as He called them to be incorporated into Himself. The influence of His Incarnation was not a diffusive sanctification of mankind, but an inclusive sanctification of human nature, so that those into whom His Humanity is infused as a regenerating instrument become new creatures in Him, and are raised out of the corruptions of the old world.[45]

The incorporation is not effected by subjective movements in the believer's heart but by concrete covenanted acts which are the divine means by which the body of Christ grows. Fr. Benson firmly re-establishes baptism in the primacy it has in the New Testament and the creeds and from which later tradition tended to displace it as the sacrifice of the Mass was given a more dominant place—'*the* Blessed Sacrament'. As a true Tractarian he did not allow that the practice of infant baptism gave grounds for that tentative, vestigial understanding of regeneration which was so prevalent in the Church. But there is a difference between his teaching and that of Pusey. In an article on 'The Mystical Theology of Fr. Benson' Fr. Geoffrey Curtis CR points out that 'Pusey teaches emphatically that every sin after baptism so weakens the effect of the grace of baptism that he who has once fallen from this grace can nevermore reach the same position as he who has kept the white robe of baptism unspotted. Conversion he describes as a slow process which can only partly restore the health engendered by baptism.'[45] With Fr. Benson there is as great an emphasis on the reality of regeneration in the baptismal gift of the Spirit; it is 'a complete Deific act'. 'The Spirit . . . by reason of His Procession from the Eternal Son, flows forth not merely upon the creatures, but into the depth of the nature of such as are regenerated in Him.'[47] But it is not complete in the rather static sense of Pusey's thought, rather complete as the initiation of a process of transformation. 'The infusion of Christ's Humanity is a developing gift capable of nourishment and increase, confirmation, edification, for it is correspondent with our human nature, and Christ is to be "formed within us" gradually.'[48]

The Eucharist is an essential element in this process, sustaining and renewing baptismal union with Christ. It goes without saying that he rejected the attitude of conventional Protestantism which reduced the Eucharist to a 'memorial of something done long ago'; but he was equally critical of the eucharistic practice of Roman Catholicism which tended to encourage the fantasy of a local Presence in spite of the safeguards and nuances of its official theology, and was suggestive of a view of the sacrament as 'the appointed means of bringing a Saviour down to us to visit and console us'. For him the 'movement' of the Eucharist is not the descending of Christ to be 'available' to man but that of the *sursum corda*, the elevation into substantial identity with his glorified body of the earthly elements, the power of the Holy Spirit effecting their assimilation, and the corresponding raising up into union with himself of those who feed upon them. He refers to the incidents of Christ eating after his Resurrection as throwing light on the Eucharist. 'We see by faith how His Body taking these earthly things, as when He fed on the broiled fish, absorbs them into itself, and makes its glorious power to stream forth through that which it assumes and gathers us as we feed thereon into its own supernatural majesty.'[49] He did not believe that the doctrine of Transubstantiation properly safeguarded the truth of the Real Presence and regarded the corollary of the doctrine which states that the body of Christ is withdrawn once digestion begins as a fatal error. For him an account of the Real Presence which fails to show the glorified body of Christ as 'abiding in the faithful as their perpetual nourishment' stands self-condemned. It ruins the very principle of the unity of the Church which consists in the bond of substantial union provided by the abiding, inherent presence of the body of Christ in believers; without this there is only an agglomeration of individuals. Instead of being caught up on the controversies of western theology Fr. Benson theologizes in a way which antedates the rise of scholasticism and instinctively reproduces the themes typical of the eastern tradition in its unbroken continuity with the patristic vision. Thus he naturally gives great attention to the role of the Spirit in the Eucharist.

As at first by His Power the Body of Christ was formed at the Incarnation, so by Him it is given at the consecration. And it is by His Power we are able to feed upon it. Had He not been dwelling in us we might have received the outer forms and yet we could not have been in any sense partakers of the Body and Blood of Christ . . . . And as we received our communion the Blessed Spirit gave us our resurrection body; and He gave us fresh impulses of His own personal presence; He laid hold of us with a firmer grasp seeking to enable us with new power to live unto God.[50]

We take this Pentecostal understanding of the Eucharist for granted in eastern Orthodoxy; in the liturgy of St. John Chrysostom the worshippers sing after communion 'we have seen the true light, we have received the heavenly Spirit . . . etc.' but it is not common in western spirituality.

Again in expounding the nature of sin, contrition and absolution in terms of the vital presence and personal action of the indwelling Spirit Fr. Benson shows his freedom from the heavily juridical idiom of Latin moral theology which would be borrowed uncritically in some circles in the next phase of the Catholic

movement. Sin for the Christian is not so much the infringement
of an external law as primarily 'grieving the Holy Spirit' whose
indwelling in us through baptism is not an inert presence but an
active personal involvement with us. He is engaged with us in a
strife of intense love as we resist.

> We must think of this struggle of the Spirit of God with our soul in its
> tenderness of love. He was not struggling with us for a display of power,
> not as a man struggles with wild beasts. He was struggling with the
> tenderness of love, as a parent with a child. When He was struggling with
> our nature His love suffered wounds. He suffered by the wounds He saw
> us inflicting on ourselves. Each sin we did was a grief to this Blessed
> Spirit, Who has thus been struggling with us all this time . . . . It
> belongs to the impassible nature of Almighty God that He cannot be
> wounded; nevertheless, by the mystery of the Incarnation, as identified
> with the incarnate Word the Holy Ghost has vibrated as with nerves of
> sympathy in response of pain for every sin we have done.[51]

Contrition then is an 'energy of the work of the Holy Ghost'
rousing the soul to mourn by a deepened awareness of this
wounded love, and it manifests itself not by a bitter revulsion
from self, but in a 'flame of love' which 'will break the heart
indeed, and yet it is the instrument of a mysterious tenderness of
joy'.[52] We are reminded of the teaching of the early monastic
Fathers such as St. John Climacus on 'joy-giving grief'. When this
inspired contrition is expressed in confession the absolution of
the priest is no mere formal exercise of ecclesiastical authority; it
is the 'voice of the anointing Spirit' and its effect is not dispensa-
tion from a penalty but the reopening in the heart of the 'well of
water springing up into eternal life' which has become choked.

If the sacraments are indeed not mere ecclesiastical ordinances
but covenanted, vitalizing acts of the Holy Spirit renewing the
Church in Christ then this invests any depreciation of them with a
terrible significance. When Fr. Benson spoke about Satanic attack
on the Church he meant not so much direct assault as the parasitic
growth of spurious forms of Christianity in which the religious
instincts of mankind are satisfied but the communication of
divine grace is cut off. 'Christ ordained His sacraments as His
means of giving this power to His people, and, therefore, such
simulating forms of Christianity as Satan originates will be
chiefly to be recognized by their setting aside or mutilating the
sacraments of grace.'[53] The opposition to the development of the

sacramental life in the Anglican Church through the Oxford
Movement was only to be expected, as was the apparent flourishing of the sects; 'the carnal heart has such a shrinking from
sacramental grace . . . Sacraments can be tolerated as empty
signs, but the moment that we acknowledge a Divine Presence
within them there is no limit to their claim'.[54]

THE THEOLOGY OF PRAYER

How little do we think of it as a real substantive truth that in order to pray
we are taken into the very being of God; that this is no mere philosophical
idea, no mere metaphor, no mere phrase, but that more truly than we
speak with our lips we speak with the utterance of the Second Person of
the blessed Trinity, and more truly than our words go forth to vibrate on
the lower air, our words go forth to fill the ear of the eternal Father with
the utterance of His only begotten Son.[55]

Fr. Benson's teaching on prayer illustrates more strikingly
than anything else the radical theocentricity of his mind. His
almost exclusive concern is to expound prayer in every one of its
manifestations and aspects as a participation in the communion
between the Son and the Father in the power and energy of the
Holy Spirit. This unwavering focus on the divine life rather than
on the human religious practice does away with the dichotomy
between mystical and liturgical prayer, personal and 'official'
prayer which is so often taken for granted. The quotation above is
in fact concerned with the recitation of the daily office. His vision
is a unified, inclusive one. In speaking of the gift of the Holy
Spirit he writes 'The whole life of the faithful by the power of this
anointing is a life of prayer. Prayer includes all.'[56]

His doctrine of prayer can be seen in perspective by considering
it first as an aspect of the theology of the Spirit and then by
considering the office of Christ as mediator, intercessor and head
of the body.

If prayer is our speech to God it is a 'return to Him of that Voice
whereby He has already spoken to us'. This voice to us is no mere
message but is his actual self-communication to us as Holy Spirit
and so the love which is the voice of prayer is no mere 'interior
affection of our own' but 'the utterance of the indwelling Spirit of
Almighty God' as given by Christ. 'The Word of God takes such
possession of the being, that at last the intelligent creature finds

itself bursting the bond of creation, and rising up in return of gratitude with the very Being of the Creator.'[57] Our role in prayer is not to try to raise ourselves to God by the violence of natural effort but to surrender, to co-operate in the movement by which the Holy Spirit rises to the Father.

He lifts us up towards God because the eternal Father is the object to which He is continually tending; by His own eternal property He is ever proceeding from the Father to the Son, and returning from the Son to the Father, as He is the circulating bond of union between the Father and the Son. Now He dwells in the humanity of Christ, but He cannot break away from this law of the divine life; He cannot constrain Himself from this circulating tendency which is His divine law of action as the Third Person of the Blessed Trinity. But He takes up that humanity into the same stream of divine action; by the same tendency of His Being He lifts up the manhood of the Son and presents it to the Father. He cannot be anywhere without hastening back to the Father . . . And as He takes us up into that manhood, He carries us up also with this irrepressible tendency which is nothing else but the eternal flow of the stream of eternal love toward the Father, who is the fount of all love.[58]

This view of prayer as the presentation of the manhood of Christ to the Father gives a firm foundation to his intense personal devotion to Jesus and makes his understanding of the high priesthood and mediation of Christ very vivid. Christ is our high priest, not as an external Intercessor supplicating on man's behalf. Rather he distributes, individualizes his own comprehensive and all-sufficient prayer throughout the members of his Body; 'they are . . . so many mouths to Himself; and as they pray for themselves, His voice fills their utterance with the authority and claim belonging to Himself'.[59]

His theology of contemplation is equally Christocentric. Contemplation is not an abstraction from the humanity of Christ. It is indeed gazing on the ascended Christ, a gaze which admits us into the joy of his perfected manhood. Contemplation is through and through a loving of Jesus and precisely insofar as it is this it passes on with the gaze of Jesus into the infinite heights of communion with the Father. It is Jesus we gaze on but 'the Father does not regard the love of Christ as if it were a shortcoming which is unable to extend itself towards the Divine Majesty, and therefore rests upon the throne of Christ as an inferior object. It is quite the reverse. The love which rises up to Christ cannot stop short in

Christ. It must reach to the Father's Person, for He is in the
Father and the Father in Him.'[60] In gazing on Jesus we are borne
on in the flow of his entire being towards the Father. The sheer
simplicity and apparent repose of 'looking to Jesus' is in a sense
deceptive. It is a case of feeling becoming 'so intense that it is no
longer felt'.[61] There is in this repose energy and ecstatic motion
into the depths of God. 'We may perhaps seem to be resting while
we are gazing upon Him. We are quite unaware that He is trans-
porting us in ecstasies of motion far more powerful than anything
that we have been through before.'[62]

THE CHURCH

Chapter 7 on Church and Mission in the teaching of Fr. Benson
makes clear how alien to him was the nostalgia for the 'ages of
faith' which is popularly attributed to the men of the Oxford
Movement, and everything which is suggested by the modern
term 'triumphalism'. When he does look back it is to the confessing Church of the pre-Constantinian era in its freedom from
'harlot union with temporal power' and from reliance on elabor-
ate structures. But he regarded the attitude which looked to the
Church of a past age as normative as nearly sacrilegious. 'No age
suffices to present to our view the Church of God in her completeness; no country, no age can do this. The Church cannot be seen
in the completeness of her organic life as the Bride of Christ until
the heavenly Jerusalem shall be seen descending out of heaven
from God.'[63] Catholicity is primarily an eschatological concept,
the fullness and universality which will finally be disclosed as the
outcome of the Church's pilgrimage through history and the
assimilation into the body of Christ of the successive generations.
'We may see how the varying manifestations of the Church of
Christ in the several countries of Christendom and in the various
periods of her history are accomplishing destinies of the highest
importance [since] it has its own proper development from age to
age, and each generation must furnish that which is necessary to
the completeness of the body of Christ'.[64] He had a strong sense
of the relativity of the forms in which the Church has been
constituted and its need to be ready to abandon structures and
methods sometimes regarded as indispensable. 'We are never to
suppose that anything is essential to His Church because it has

been a source of strength whereon we have relied in times gone by.' 'Christ has not promised stationary permanence to His Church.'[65]

Even in the course of this short chapter it can clearly be seen that no-one could have a higher doctrine of the Church. It is rooted in the very nature of man. 'The kingdom of Christ is . . . not a mere congregation gathered together by external agency. It is an upspringing organism which indicates a latent vitality in human nature called into energy by the Voice of Jesus, the true Son of Man.'[66] It is the body of Christ, the supernatural sphere of man's deification, a divine organism animated by the Holy Spirit. Yet equally true and important is that the Church is weak. If it is the extension of the Incarnation it is bound to embody the features of the Lord's incarnate life—vulnerability, homelessness and poverty. This glorious weakness can only be lived out when the Church is a community of contemplative faith sustained by direct dependence on the invisible head and living in the unseen Spirit. As soon as the tension of this gaze of faith is relaxed the Church has to fall back on substitute security based on human resources and organization and forfeits the true strength which lies in weakness. The most obvious example was the attempt to make the lines of authority converge on a visible focus in the papacy, rather than on Christ the invisible head. Writing in the aftermath of the First Vatican Council (1869–70), Fr. Benson insisted that the effort to guarantee truth and unity in this way was self-defeating and divisive as was shown by the fragmentation of Christendom from the schism between east and west onwards. He held that the extreme centralization of authority in Rome was not only wrong in principle but would be found impossible to sustain in the face of the truly world-wide expansion of the Church through modern missions.

As we see in R. M. C. Jeffery's chapter Fr. Benson deplored the tendency to represent the ministry as a separate caste from the laity, exercising an exclusive prerogative of authority delegated by an absent Lord. Christ exercises his authority in the Church by endowing it corporately with his Spirit. One manifestation of this authority is the collegial authority of the episcopate. Looking back over the process which had culminated in the declaration of papal infallibility, Fr. Benson wrote of the early decay of the original conciliar principle: 'The spiritual idea of Catholicity, all bishops being one by reason of the one Spirit Who spoke through each individually, and then correctively through all collectively, that which is set before us in Ephesians iv, died out, and the machinery alone seemed to remain.'[67] He welcomed every movement towards collegial episcopal action as in the convening of the first Lambeth Conference, and every advance towards synodical government at diocesan level. But balancing this high regard for the representative authority of the bishops and clergy was his insistence that the laity were also important agents of the teaching authority of the Holy Spirit.

The Holy Spirit dwells in the Church collectively, for we are all brethren as being born again by the operation of the Blessed Spirit. As He dwells in the Church universal, He can speak by any member of the Church at any time . . . . When he speaks He can make His voice to be heard though He chooses to speak by a person of the greatest insignificance. He dwells in all, and can speak by any and can cause that no word spoken by His inspiration shall fall to the ground.[68]

Taking a stand against the sort of expectation fostered by Ultramontanism Fr. Benson taught that the notion that the Church was constantly able to pronounce on the issues which confront it through an official *magisterium* was quite unwarranted. He recognized the importance of the stimulus given to the organic development of doctrine by the need to counteract heretical teaching, but he does not allow that the effect of the Paraclete's guidance of the church is to be reckoned in terms of an ever-growing body of doctrine. The promise of Christ 'does not imply that the Holy Ghost will make fresh points clear, or formulate fresh utterances of orthodoxy as time goes on. Such decisions, when legitimately made by the Church, are doubtless a result of His guidance; but His guidance is rather practical so that the whole body of revealed truth, as a living entity, may become the rule of our life with joyous and sanctifying experience.'[69]

The theological concept of 'tradition' does not appear very much in an explicit way in Fr. Benson's writings but his account of the way revealed truth is maintained as a living flame by the Holy Spirit through the ages closely resembles the pneumatological and dynamic approach to tradition found in the best representatives of Orthodox theology.

THE CONSUMMATION

There is in Fr. Benson's theology no resolution of the tension between the Pauline theme of the consummation of all creation in Christ and the traditional doctrine of hell which he propounded with a forcefulness which, typically, caused the young Henry Scott Holland to walk out of a retreat he was conducting. But if Fr. Benson spoke against the rise amongst a new generation of churchmen of the belief that in the end all men would be saved, he was equally critical of those who misrepresented God as a sadistic avenger by dwelling on images of punitive suffering. His doctrine of heaven and hell is bound up with his dynamic view of human nature. Man is in a constant state of growth and development in which habitual acts intensify and consolidate his character for good or ill. On the one hand life towards God and especially faithfully endured suffering opens up ever greater capacities for him:

. . . vast chasms of void darkness as receptacles of the glorious light which is to be our eternal portion.[70]

Every act of love will have left in the heart a craving of love which could not be satisfied without that reward and a capacity of love which that reward shall abundantly satisfy . . . The energies of the divine life are not merely transient and successive, but permanent in such a manner as to manifest a continuous growth. Every act that is done in the power of the divine life is not merely an instance of its exercise, but a fresh development in him that does it of the divine nature whereby alone it can be done.[71]

The life to come will not be a reward in the sense of an external recompense, it will be the germination and fruition of this life. Likewise hell is not a place of banishment but the condition of those whose lives develop irrevocably away from God, 'the riot of moral energies driven onward madly in fruitless agitation'.[72] 'The soul formed in God's image needs no torture. It must agonize in its own cravings'.[73]

As we might expect, his biblical and Hebraic cast of mind made him suspect 'underlying Manicheism' beneath conventional teaching on the immortality of the soul. The mysterious hope of the resurrection of the body was of intense concern to him. Here Christianity showed its radical difference from 'Oriental philosophies' which 'look to man's perfection by eliminating his spiritual being from its material surroundings'.[74] Christian asceticism was inspired not by the prospect of laying aside the senses but by the prospect of their transfiguration so as to participate in the total experience of God in the risen life; 'they are given as germs of the resurrection power, and must be rendered up to the work of Christ now, in order that they may henceforth lay hold of Him as the true object for which they were formed.'[75]

As Fr. Benson's theology reaches its climax in the vision of the world to come all the distinctive features of his spirit make themselves felt. Typically it has a twin focus in two great images of tremendous movement—the coming of Christ and the coming forth of the Holy City from God. A vivid expectation of the second Advent fills his letters, sermons and prayers but it did not hang on that return to earthly conditions imagined by sectarian apocalyptic. The theme remains a mysterious and potent image rather than a hard and fast doctrinal datum. (He wrote that 'the Irvingites unhappily crystallized and froze up the idea of Christ's second coming when they gave it its true place as the one object of Christian contemplation. But if with them the fountain became a hard mass of shining ice to dazzle rather than nourish, with most of us the thought is a fountain that does not flow at all.')[76] The second Advent is not a movement in space, a coming to us, 'so much as a coming forth from within us, showing Himself truly within us, perfecting our faculties that we may apprehend that which is beyond our thought while we are here. The appearing is a revelation, so that when He is revealed, we shall also be revealed with Him in His glory, and He at His coming will be glorified in His saints and we in Him.'[77]

So the final coming of Christ and the coming forth of the Holy City, the Communion of Saints, is one and the same, the ultimate manifestation by the Holy Spirit of the whole Christ, the glorified collective Christ. 'All that comes forth from God has its origin in the Procession of the Holy Ghost. The coming forth of the Holy City from God is the final and crowning operation of the Holy Ghost.'[78] He glories in the dynamic language of coming and coming forth because it suggests the life of the world to come as an eternal movement by which the saints penetrate ever further into the divine life. He takes the image of the pilgrimage of the people of God and projects it into eternity. 'In this glorious lustre of Divine Righteousness, by the power of the Holy Spirit, shall the City go forth on its mysterious march of eternal triumph. The Spirit of God proceeding from the Father and the Son makes this City to go forth. The Spirit of God has upborne us here on many a weary pilgrimage and He will bear us on in this glorious march of Eternal Light.'[79]

In his doctrine of the Communion of Saints and the beatific vision he brings into play all his resources of expression to point to the fulfilment of man's social nature in the reciprocal love and coinherence of the saints in glory and their participation in the Trinitarian interchange, yet all is simply Christocentric. 'It is in seeing Christ that we attain to the vision of God'.[80] And far from losing sight of the cross of Calvary he plants its enduring love at the heart of the consummated creation.

The love whereby the man Christ Jesus dwells in the bosom of the eternal glory, is the bond which preserves the order of the new creation—the power which energizes in the functions of the new creation. The love of His Heart thrills through all His Body,—all the company of His elect,— with a never-failing Pulsation. Continually does He present Himself to the Father in the integrity of that atoning power, by which on Calvary He broke through the gates of the grave. Were this self-oblation of Jesus for a moment wanting, the whole constitution of that Heavenly Jerusalem would be immediately dissolved . . . . Without a perpetual offering it would cease to be a Temple. But now it lives for ever in the sympathy of the crucified Son of God.[81]

3
Bruising the Serpent's Head: Father Benson and the Atonement

A. M. Ramsey

READERS of Fr. Benson's letters and books of meditation cannot fail to notice his vivid sense of the unity of the cross and the Resurrection. He sees the Passion with the light of Easter upon it and he urges us to understand the Resurrection only in terms of faith in the crucified. 'Christ triumphed upon the Cross that we might go through death to victory, not that we might pass to victory without enduring death. Our victory can only be the victory of the dead. Only in proportion as we are dead with Christ can we share His victory. We little know how our eagerness for success thwarts the manifestation of the Resurrection power by which alone the truly mortified life is to be perfected.'[1] The ceaseless rejoicing of Christians with the ascended Jesus in the heavenly places has as its counterpart their no less ceaseless dying to the world. The aim of this chapter is to probe into the theology which lies beneath this recurring theme of Benson's teaching and spirituality.

Benson's more concentrated thought about the doctrine of the Atonement is found in three parts of his writings. There is the volume of sermons with the title *Redemption,* published in 1861 a few years before the inception of the Cowley community. There is the exposition of the *Epistle to the Romans,* 1891. And, perhaps most illuminating of all, there is the series of articles in the American Anglo-Catholic magazine *The Church Eclectic* published in Milwaukee. These articles appeared between 1894 and 1897 and the list of them runs:

December 1894	The Atoning Triumph of the Incarnate Word
June 1896	The Doctrine of the Atonement
August 1896	The Conquest of the Arch Enemy
September 1896	The One Great Sacrifice

These articles, with the heading 'By the Rev. R. M. Benson, M.A., Student of Christ Church, Oxford, and Mission Priest of St. John the Evangelist, Boston,' have a concentration and a continuity akin to a treatise. They give mature expression to a theme which had been peeping out in some of Benson's volumes, especially those of *The Final Passover*.

The work entitled *Redemption* is a good introduction to Benson's thought about Atonement. It contains a series of sermons preached in St. Thomas's Church in Oxford in Lent and Eastertide 1860, together with some other sermons, all arranged as a consecutive treatise. Sacrifice is presented not as an action contingent upon human sinfulness but as a true relation between man as creature and God as creator. 'Sacrifice . . . the sacrifice of praise, is coeval with creation . . . . When the sons of God shouted for joy, their song of praise was . . . the sacrifice of their whole being to Him from Whom it came, and in that sacrifice they found their joy.' But 'in a world of sin there can be no oblation to God, unless the ties are broken which bind the offerer to that world which sin has separated from God'.[2] Hence when Christ came to be man's true sacrifice in a world of sin, suffering and death, 'the sacrifice of praise . . . offered by the spotless Son of God in a world of sinners had to lift up the whole burden of the sin of man before it could be uttered in the proper accents of joy'.[3] In this context the penal aspect comes in: 'Let us not shrink from believing in the sacrifice of Christ as a satisfaction of God's offended justice'.[4] But the satisfaction was far more than a retrospective transaction; it was a victorious new creation. 'The righteousness of Christ is not a mere negative justice—an absence of evil. It is a creative righteousness . . . by calling up a new creation filled with Divine righteousness'.[5] So there follows the Resurrection. Risen and ascended, Christ is now the perfect sacrifice, the gift from God to man and the gift from man to God.

He is himself the sacrifice which gives meaning to the Eucharist, and God's justification of sins is the bringing of men to share in his own righteousness through the risen Christ. But the faith whereby we live in the risen Christ is a continuing death to the world.

Such is the theme of the sermons in the volume *Redemption*. We shall find further development in Benson's later writings, but *Redemption* is in its own time a work remarkable for depth and comprehensiveness. In one way it resembles F. D. Maurice's *The Doctrine of Sacrifice*, where sacrifice is related to the creature-creator relationship and to a divine pattern in the world. In another way it resembles McCleod Campbell's *The Nature of the Atonement*. Campbell wrote of the need 'to see the Atonement in its own light', meaning that while Christ bore our penalty he bore it so utterly in his own way that to call his suffering penalty is misleading. Benson is near to Campbell when he writes 'He bore punishment, but He bore it not as punishment. What had been punishment in us, in Him was voluntary effort'. But he is again near to Maurice when he continues '"He emptied Himself" of Godhead, and "became obedient unto death". In this position he served God with an entire self-sacrifice, the sacrifice not merely of a dependent creature, the very law of whose life is sacrifice, but the sacrifice of the self-existent Creator.'[6]

The *Exposition of the Epistle to the Romans* has some portions which deserve better than the neglect which the work has in general received. There is a curious, but not unplausible, suggestion about the origins of the Church in Rome as a background to the Epistle. Benson pictures the first Christians in Rome not as a community but as groups who after being converted at Pentecost returned from Jerusalem to Rome and were followers of Christ with little knowledge or understanding of the new faith. To them St. Paul writes to expound the fundamentals, not as to people who ought to know better like the Galatians but as to people who have had no chance of knowing better. To St. Paul the old Jewish faith and the new Christianity are really one religion, the seed and the flower; hence the optimism of his pleas for the conversion of his fellow Jews in chapters 9, 10 and 11 of the Epistle.

It is in this work that we can study Benson's understanding of the biblical terms. Justification does not merely attribute to believers a legal condition of righteousness but actually brings God's own righteousness to them through their share in the risen life of Christ. While Benson is thus far nearer to J. H. Newman than to the contemporary evangelicals on this theme, his thought seems to come from his own study of scripture rather than from the post-reformation controversies and definitions. On the well-known crux in Romans 3:25, 'whom God set forth to be a propitiation', Benson takes *hilasterion* to mean the mercy seat, the lid of the ark; and he goes deep into a typology of the ark and the mercy seat in relation to Christ as both concealing and revealing the presence of God. As might be expected there is a very Bensonian treatment of baptism into the death of Christ in Romans 6. Not only the death but the burial also is a continuing process for the Christian believer through the whole of his life.

The themes found in *Redemption* and in his *Exposition of Romans* recur in many places in Benson's writings, the note of '*Christus Victor*' being everywhere prominent. When however we come to the American articles written in the nineties we are conscious that some development in his thought has been happening. While he had used the penal concept, albeit with the reserves and modifications which we saw in *Redemption,* he came vehemently to repudiate the influence of that theory as incompatible with the doctrine he wishes to commend. Several times we find him writing in this vein: 'it is to be feared that much evil of a very practical character arises from the commixture of false ideas which have no warrant in Holy Scripture with the great doctrine of the Atonement. Subsidiary features which were the groundwork of much speculation in ancient times have usurped the place of prominence so that . . . the primary Scripture doctrine of the conquest of Satan by the Seed of the Woman . . . gives place to a transaction whereby man is to be made at one with God, not by deliverance from Satan's power and the gift of new life . . . but by a judicial process of *substituted suffering* which enables men to gain a suppositious reconciliation with God, having escaped the condemnation of an abstract justice.'[7] It seems that Benson's mind was haunted by this contrast. 'The Passion has been made void of its glory. It has been represented as a degradation accepted for the vindication of God's Majesty by visiting man's sin upon man as a sinner instead of being recognized as a Divine Self-assertion enabling man to conquer Satan, that God might be glorified over the arch-fiend and man might rise in triumph over his tyranny.'[8]

It is in the series of essays in *The Church Eclectic* that Benson's theme of 'Christus Victor' is found in mature and powerful expression. The Atonement originates in the omnipotence of God the creator whose mighty power restores the creation which Satan had deranged. Man has become subject to suffering and death. As long as man is in the world he is sinful, ruled by Satan, and having death as his inevitable lot. God has however been preparing for man's deliverance, a deliverance not apart from man but by man and through man. Throughout his exposition Benson puts great emphasis upon the prophecies of redemption made to Eve in the Book of Genesis with the prediction that the woman, after bearing much suffering at the hands of Satan, will one day bruise the serpent's head. It is fitting that the deliverance of man should be wrought by one who is man. So the incarnate Son of God comes to do battle against Satan with the weapons of love and obedience. Christ suffers in realizing the intense hatred of the divine holiness against sin as he makes himself one with sinners, but his sufferings are not penal since they flow from his obedient will and issue in victory. Christ suffers no less from the onslaught of Satan upon humanity and upon himself. But by dying to sin and to the world he lives the life that is life indeed.

So Benson writes 'Satan stored up all the hatred of mankind against Him, and himself in Gethsemane struggled against Him with such intense fury, seeking to show that there was some element of moral weakness . . . unequal to the task of redemption, some element that would give way in the tremendous sufferings of the conflict. So it was that the powers of darkness came round about the Cross until they retreated, absolutely baffled. The Son of God came to struggle with Satan and to endure all that Satan could do to make him swerve from the simple law of loving obedience.'[9] Christ by his death glorified the Father, said No to Satan, died to the world and was raised to the life which is man's true life. The risen Christ brings righteousness and life to those who accept it by a faith which means a continual dying to the world so that the creator's omnipotence is vindicated in the created world through man.

In working out this theme Benson again and again meditates around the imagery of the seed of the woman bruising the serpent's head. In his musings around this context he ranges over large areas of thought and experience. Suffering is indeed the penalty of sin not in the sense that God inflicts it upon sinners as a punishment but in the sense that it is the outcome of Satan's disastrous work. While therefore Christ suffered in his oneness with sinful humanity, the greatest emphasis is upon the suffering of Christ's exposure to Satan and Satan's onslaught upon himself. Benson also meditates upon both Isaiah 53 and Psalm 22 in depicting the mental suffering of Christ in his conflict and the victorious outcome. In the further essays on 'Scriptural Teaching about Redemption' he examines some of the biblical phrases and argues against a penal interpretation of them. For instance 'the Blood of Christ is our ransom, not because it was forfeited in death by a substitutional penalty which he endured but because it energized in life by a Divine power of which the outward death of the Body could not deprive it'. 'We are too apt to think as if . . . the death of Christ was a misfortune, however triumphant in its issues, instead of being the most glorious manifestation of Divine power which the universe has to adore.' 10

The thought which is set out in a consecutive pattern in the American essays had already appeared more sporadically in the volumes of *The Final Passover* a few years earlier; and a little later than the American essays there came the exposition of the Psalter in the two volumes of *The War Songs of the Prince of Peace* (1901). Here the Psalter is seen as a kind of epic of the Messiah's conflict and victory over evil. Indeed Benson's theme resembles more closely than does any other treatise on the Atonement the words of Newman's hymn in the *Dream of Gerontius*:

O wisest love, that flesh and blood
Which did in Adam fail,
Should strive afresh against the foe,
Should strive and should prevail.

Some may wonder why, in the light of Benson's teaching on the divine victory, his sense of hostility to the world continues so strongly. There is little of the doctrine, familiar in the East, of the cosmos being recreated by the power of the Resurrection, for to Benson the world is still the enemy to be died to. On the other hand the transfiguring of persons and of sufferings is a recurring theme of teaching and meditation. Concerning the world as it once was and the world as it now is there is a luminous discussion in *The Final Passover* in connection with John 16:8, the Spirit convicting the world, and John 16:33, Christ overcoming the world. The world as the organism of sinful humanity hostile to God has been deprived of its power, and by dying to it we can live in freedom from it; but the world still remains as a snare until the Lord will return and his kingdom will be all in all.

There are some who will be ready to absorb Benson's teaching as it stands with only a little paraphrasing; there are others who may be repelled by the imagery of the bruising of the serpent's head and may cry out for 'demythologizing'. This, however, may not be too difficult, for sin is indeed monstrous and tyrannical in its grip upon the human race, and deliverance from it can only be at terrible cost. The good news of Christianity is that the cost has been borne by God himself in such a way that to believe and to share in what God has done is to know a powerful and contagious freedom.

4
Richard Benson: Man of the Bible

M. Gibbard SSJE

FATHER Benson had just crossed the Atlantic. He stood by an open porthole looking, entranced as so many have, at the Sandy Rock Lighthouse, the entrance of the Lower New York Bay, and the city beyond. He sat down and wrote to a friend:

I have been keeping the voyage in active company with King David, and learning some little more of the delight of that inexhaustible trea- sury. . . . Only one does wish that one could make people round about know something of the happiness that they might have in the Psalter if they would. . . . It makes one wonder why God should have been pleased to reveal such a delight to oneself. One ought to be very thankful.

Then he added with, I guess, a twinkle in his eye, but not quite fairly:

I think the joy of Holy Scripture is very much hidden by the joylessness of commentators who write about it with no sense of the supernatural delight.[1]

He was ever a lover of the Bible—from first to last. His gover- ness told that he always before going to sleep used to read from a small New Testament given to him by his mother. One night his nanny found him lying on the floor. When she told him to get into bed, he stubbornly refused. So his father came, sat him on his knee and asked what it was all about. Richard pointed to his passage for that night: 'Thou therefore endure hardness as a good soldier of Jesus Christ' and asked, 'How shall I endure hardness, if I cannot sleep on the floor?'[2]

They were a well-to-do family. Husband and wife had both been brought up in the firmly evangelical Clapham sect, under the influence of John Venn. While Richard's elder brother was sent to Harrow, he was educated at home. As her youngest child, he was always close to his mother. Doubtless it was from her that he received a deep, evangelical love of the text of the Bible. Mother and son together published in 1856 a book of their poetry, *Lays of Memory, Sacred and Social.* He remained a lifelong versifier. There are lines in this book which hint at a link between them, which might even echo Augustine's intimacy with his mother Monica shortly before her death at Ostia[3]:

Gazing together there, we oft have felt
  In mutual converse that the saints on high
Were nearer than if now on Earth they dwelt.[4]

PUSEY AND BENSON

After making two unsuccessful efforts for a scholarship at Balliol, a college then climbing to its intellectual eminence, Richard Benson came up to Oxford as an undergraduate in the autumn of 1844 to Christ Church. His life might have turned out very differently, had he been successful at Balliol. For it was at Christ Church that he came under the influence of Dr Pusey; this was momentous for him. Benson took a second class in classics and in mathematics, the only two honour schools in those days. But far more important for him was that he started Hebrew under Dr Pusey. Soon he was elected on Pusey's nomination a Student of Christ Church and went on to win the Kennicott Hebrew scholarship.

  Fifteen years or so earlier Pusey, after two periods of study in Germany, had written his first book, on *The Rationalist Character lately predominant in the Theology of Germany.* He had deplored the lengths to which a critical study of the Bible had gone in Germany. But a significant word in his title was 'lately', for he had detected a more orthodox and a more spiritual tendency in the theological climate there. He himself had gone so far as to concede that the scriptures were not uniformly inspired, insisting that since the imparting of *religious* truth is the object of biblical revelation, it could not be maintained 'that even historical passages, in which no religious truth was contained, were *equally* inspired with the rest, and consequently, that no error, however minute, could even here be admitted'.[5] He had felt uneasy at the

time about this concession and he had written in a letter 'I expect
to be thought one-third mystic, one-third sceptic, and one-third
(which will be thought the worst imputation of all) a Methodist,
though I am none of the three.'[6] Very soon he withdrew even this
small concession to the critical studies of the scriptures. He then
maintained an inflexibly traditional position throughout his fifty-
three years as professor of Hebrew. In his will he declared that his
first book must never be re-published.

Five years before Benson came up to Christ Church, Pusey
suffered a blow, which permanently turned him in on himself.
This was the death of his wife. He had had the frustrations of ten
years' forbidden courtship and then eleven years of deep compan-
ionship in married life. His wife's early death Pusey regarded as
God's punishment for his sins and he bitterly reproached himself
for his slight flirtation with German liberal theology. After her
death he said he never raised his eyes when crossing the quad of
Christ Church, because he could never forget the pall on his
wife's coffin as it fluttered there in the wind. As penance he
imposed a forbidding burden on himself—for example, 'to ask
myself before reading anything whether it was God's will that I
should read it'; 'to avoid excitement or jesting, except when with
children'; 'to make the fire to me from time to time the type of
hell'.[7]

This was the Pusey, whose influence on Benson was so deep
and enduring. During the last two years of Pusey's life Fr.
Benson, even with all his own responsibilities as superior and as
parish priest, continued to go, whenever possible, to Pusey's
lectures on the Hebrew Bible.[8] Fr. Benson treasured sacred
memories of hours he spent as a pupil in Pusey's study; almost
fifty years afterwards he could write of them, when Liddon's
biography of Pusey was coming out:

Even with Liddon's pen the true memories of that study in Tom Quad
could never be brought to light. The things which could be told would
have been to the things that can never be told, only as the skull to the
countenance radiant with beauty, and life, and love.[9]

First his mother and then Dr Pusey were probably the strongest
influences on his life; so we are not surprised to see the love of the
Bible running through his life like a thread of gold.

MINISTRY AND COMMUNITY

We can trace this love of the scriptures both in his ministry as a parish priest — he was for thirty-six years an indefatigable parish priest — and also as founder and inspirer of his community.

First, he saw the value of corporate Bible reading in the work of the ministry. Perhaps this came from his evangelical family background. He wrote in 1874 to Fr. O'Neill, one of his closest followers, then in India:

I am very glad that you have adopted the practice of an hour's daily reading of Holy Scripture all together. It is most desirable. May God, indeed, bring His word home with power to all of your hearts as you carry on the study![10]

He himself had experienced — he seems to be referring to his work as a parish priest — this fruit of patient Bible reading, for he wrote about the same time, 'Some of the fruits of my ministry to which I look back with the most gratitude took nearly a twelve-month of family prayer and scripture exposition.'[11]

Next, it was his love of the Bible — particularly the Psalms — that kept the daily divine office from ever becoming for him an external burden in a busy life. 'The offices are in fact', he wrote, 'if properly used, one of the best forms of meditation and of Scripture study'.[12] He saw that this daily office would call for an effort not only of the heart and of the will in worship, but also of the understanding and so of study. 'We cannot present these words to God', he said, 'without some good understanding'.[13]

This in turn led him to lay a particular stress on biblical study for the members of his Society, because they were going to have to live, he said, in an intellectual and sceptical age. Although they were not likely to have to 'combat the intellectual giants of unbelief', they would certainly have to deal with those who 'echo the objections of greater men without themselves understanding them'. He did not wish his followers to give slick answers, but rather to be able to share with others a vision of truth.

The spirit of the age calls upon us as a Religious Society very specially to cultivate this devout habit of searching the Scriptures. Instead of merely giving an answer to unbelief, we have to gain for ourselves a vision of truth through the very dificulty at which they mock.[14]

It was *serious* study that he pressed upon his community. He wrote from the U.S.A. to a lay brother at Oxford:

I am very glad to hear of the Hebrew studies. I hope they will be serviceable to you. Although one may not, perhaps, hope to make great progress in Hebrew, yet even a little knowledge is of great value. One catches the meaning of many passages of the Old Testament which without it are almost hopeless. The construction of the language, although so simple, is so pregnant that, even more than in other languages, an adequate translation is impossible.[15]

This advice was well taken, for in the community library there is still a heavily annotated pocket version of the Hebrew Psalms, which this layman, later ordained priest, used to carry with him on his journeys.

Besides setting apart time for such study, Benson's followers were told also to

have a Bible, or portion of it, always at hand so as to be able frequently to recur to it, whether waiting for any purpose in the church or in any house.[16]

In their systematic study they were expected to work steadily and exactly like a lawyer or other professional man. He told them not to shut their eyes against (biblical) criticism:

Do not put away modern criticism as if, because it is profane, it cannot be useful. The stones of the temple were cut by foreign hands whose owners never saw Jerusalem, so will it be with the stones of the heavenly Jerusalem. Be diligent then in study and as you study modern critics let it not be to refute them in the spirit of triumph, but to see what truth is suggested by them, and where they are at fault.[17]

He himself hardly ever quoted other scholars and seldom in his writings recommended their works. In one letter he referred— with some qualification—to Bishop Westcott's commentary on St. John:

Westcott on S. John's Gospel would probably be an interesting book for you to read, treating of the philosophical basis of Christianity. We must however remember that Christianity is not a philosophy; it is an *historical fact*, quite independent of man's acceptance or rejection.[18]

For he maintained that the best commentary on scripture is scripture itself.

It is a great matter to seek for the elucidation of Bible difficulties rather from the Bible itself, than from the cleverness of critics, who are very apt to introduce thoughts by way of explanation which have no authority either from the Bible or the Creeds.[19]

'Controversy takes the place of Bible reading', he complained, 'and now we are so busy about the Bible as a book that we forget it as the Word of God.'[20] And he once wrote half-seriously, 'I often wish that every book could be burnt except the Bible and Prayer Book.'[21] He was deeply concerned that it should never be study for study's sake or for mere curiosity or still less for personal reputation.

There must be real delight in divine truth . . . . We must seek this in all our repetition of the Psalms, in all our study of Holy Scripture, in all our study of the mystery of the sacred language and in all our theological researches; we must ever be seeking to have our minds filled with this power of divine truth as a principle of supernatural life.[22]

His own commentaries and notes for meditation, all of them, have this supernatural aim. His biblical labours were always intended to lead up to meditation or mental prayer.

This, I need not say, is of the highest importance to us. It is in mental prayer that the soul really enters into union with God. No revelation however clear, no familiarity however intimate with Jesus after the flesh, no sacramental union however complete, really benefits the intelligent soul without mental prayer.[23]

In the preface to his book of meditation notes, *Benedictus Dominus*, he explained what meditation meant and how intellectual reflections though important were not the summit; and then he declared that nothing can 'take the place of *extemporaneous colloquies* of the soul with God, which are the most important part of the Meditation'.[24]

This helps us to understand Fr. Benson as a conductor of retreats and as a writer.

Throughout his years as a superior, he gave the community a month's retreat with three addresses a day, and these were steeped in the Bible. He was a voluminous writer on the scriptures. He wrote quickly, I would guess, and did not much revise what he had written. Nearly all of it was expository writing, often verse by verse commentary, to help others to reflect on and to meditate on the scriptures. He published commentaries on Proverbs 1–8, John 6 and 13–21, Romans and the Psalms. He left unpublished a manuscript on Ephesians and on a part of Job.

Amongst all his other pressing tasks, he nearly always had something on hand for his writing. When he was nearly seventy, he spent a fortnight in the Bahamas, preaching, conducting retreats, talking with individuals; and yet even there he was 'busy writing with the Hebrew Psalms before him, preparing for a new book'.[25] On his visit to India he was still pressing on with this work while staying in Calcutta.

I have had a good deal of time to work at the Psalms, but am a long way yet from finishing. The library at Bishop's College is a nice quiet place for reading; and it is pleasant with some old Hebrew books to think that they were often in the hands of Dr. Mill and Dr. Kay.[26]

When he was seventy-nine, living again in Oxford, with his eyesight failing, he wrote:

I do not see much of my fellow brothers, but I have Job for my companion in my own room, and I do not feel I want any others. I should like to get the MS ready before I die, but it seems to demand a great many revisions.[27]

Therefore it is transparently plain where Richard Benson found the heart of Christian life and the essence of the religious life in particular. Although he had made a wide study of the religious life and of the rules of many orders, he hardly ever quoted any of them. It is in the scriptures themselves that he found the inspiration for his community's life. In a similar way, a monk of our own days, Dom Bede Griffiths, who is trying to find a pattern of religious life for that India, so dear both to him and to Father Benson, has written: 'This has meant first of all a return to the Bible, on which the whole monastic tradition is based, but to the Bible interpreted in the light of the patristic tradition.'[28]

This kind of biblical study and prayer brought immense energies to Father Benson in his crowded ministry. While he was training his first companions in his community, he was also travelling all over the country for missions and retreats, he was immersed in his growing parish all day, and then praying a large part of the night—often aloud in the chapel alone—also answering ceaseless correspondence and in these quiet hours even cataloguing the library single-handed. There is an almost amusing instance of this pressure on his life. A few months before the founding of his Society, he received a letter from the Bishop of Oxford, questioning the wisdom of some very essential part of his plan. Benson excused himself from replying at once, because he was, he said, engulfed in 'the bustle and preparation for a parish fête'.

His own experience made him write: 'If we want strength for any work of God, we do well to seek it in Holy Scripture.'[29]

A fruit of his deep love of the Bible was the remarkable way he read the lessons in church. Canon Allchin has already quoted from a memoir by one who had been deeply impressed by it as a child.

The most difficult passages seemed made clear as he read them to us. No commentary beyond his wonderful intonations and inflections seemed necessary.[30]

In a similar way Fr. Page, who followed Fr. Benson as superior, wrote that people came to the community church to listen to Father Benson read the scriptures and 'by his reading to expound and interpret the sacred word'. He used to read the second lesson daily at evensong. As he grew older he read not from the lectern but from his place in choir, using a Bible with specially large print. At the end of 1904 he told Fr. Page that with his failing eyes he could manage it no longer. So on the last evening of the old year he finished reading the Apocalypse, which he loved. 'Surely I come quickly. Amen', he read, 'Come, Lord Jesus. The grace of our Lord Jesus Christ be with you all. Amen.' With these words he concluded this part of his ministry, and sat down.[31]

INSPIRATION

His use of the scriptures depended upon certain presuppositions, which few modern scholars would now accept. The question for us is how we can build up a similar effective biblical spirituality on other presuppositions. He said correctly that 'the Church has never pledged herself to any particular theory of inspiration'.[32] Yet he made his own position about the biblical writers crystal clear in his earliest commentary, *The Wisdom of the Son of David;* and from that he never changed.

They wrote not simply as their own feelings suggested, but under the *controlling* power of God the Holy Ghost. It is this controlling power which constitutes the inspiration of Holy Scripture. If we recognize Scripture as really emanating from God the Holy Ghost, although written with a very inadequate appreciation of the divine purpose, by human agency, we shall scarcely be able to avoid the acknowledgement that there must be in *all* the words of Scripture a Divine purpose and meaning, *over and above*, not contrary to or nullifying, but underlying, pervading, spiritualizing, what the writers would have intended had they merely written as men.[33]

This passage reflects the general attitude to the scriptures taken by the Fathers and by most Christian writers until the nineteenth century. It could claim a basis in some passages of holy scripture. But in my opinion it claims more for scripture than scripture in general claims for itself. St. Luke, for example, at the beginning of his gospel says no more than that he has collected the best evidence he could, and so put his gospel together.

It would appear to most modern scholars that Father Benson underestimated the human factors in the work of these inspired authors and overestimated the divine element. During his life-time many scholars abroad and in England were striving to arrive at a more adequate balance between the human and divine elements in the writing of scripture.

PSALMS

Father Benson probably regarded his two volumes on the Psalms, paradoxically entitled *The War Songs of the Prince of Peace*, and his devotional commentary on Psalm 119, entitled *The Way of Holiness*, as his most important writings. We have seen how long and hard he laboured over them. He made his own translation and tried to reproduce something of the beat and balance of the Hebrew originals.

All Fr. Benson's work on the Psalms is built upon a restrained, *typological* interpretation of the Bible, underpinned by his understanding of inspiration. He believed that the Old Testament and the New Testament were a unity, the former pointing towards and the latter proclaiming God's redeeming work in Christ for humanity. Prophecies—and also events—in the old Testament were antitypes corresponding to the type, Christ as the Redeemer of the world. In contrast to this typology Benson ruled out fanciful, allegorical interpretations—'all arbitrary manipulation of details'[34]—common as they are in the Fathers; as Ambrose, for example, commenting on the familiar verse in Psalm 72 about the king coming down 'like the rain into a fleece of wool', said that Mary was truly the fleece.[35] Though sometimes typology itself slips towards this kind of allegory, yet, as Dr Lampe has maintained, 'Allegory differs radically from the kind of typology which rests upon the perception of actual historical fulfilment.'[36]

We may notice in passing that Fr. Benson was also fascinated by a strange detailed scheme of mystical numbers, which he picked up from Dr Milo Mahan, a nineteenth-century American professor of the General Theological Seminary, New York. There is nothing quite like this scheme in the Church's tradition and many think that it does not add anything of lasting significance to Benson's commentary on the Psalter.

But through his typological interpretation Father Benson maintained that the Psalms speak so powerfully to us because they meet the whole range of hopes and fears of our human nature—created in God's image, deformed by sin, restored or at least capable of being restored through the redeeming work of Christ.

He spelt it out in the introductory chapters to *The War Songs of the Prince of Peace* in this way:

God, as He knows the diseases generated within us by the Fall, supplies us in the Psalter with that medicine which the human heart requires in order to recover its healthy action.[37]

The Psalms were inspired by God and given to us, Father Benson said,

[So] we may reach out and grasp the hand of our Deliverer. He is the True Man, the incarnate Son of God, who calls us from our own misery to share His life.[38]

The abstract and earthly idea of deliverance from enemies is transformed into the Personal consciousness of the triumphant Redeemer.[39]

The ideal set before us in the Psalter is . . . the portraiture of a representative Champion who calls us to share with Him in all that He endures because He strengthens us to follow His footsteps, and, by participation of His cross, to attain the sovereignty wherein He is glorified.[40]

Therefore it is clear that

We must see that we use the Psalter as no mere venerable tradition of ages which have passed away, but in the living fellowship of heavenly joy, whereby the children of grace ought to feel their union with the Incarnate Word.[41]

To see how this method actually works out in our use of the Psalms in worship and prayer, we could hardly do better than turn to his treatment of Psalm 63:

O God, thou art my God: early will I seek thee.
My soul thirsteth for thee; my flesh longeth after thee
In a barren and dry land where no water is.

To make the point clearer we might notice in passing how another commentator, Professor Davison, writing only some few years later, entitled the Psalm merely as 'Morning Orisons' and enquired when it could have been written by David or by some later poet.

This would not do for Fr. Benson; he boldly entitled this Psalm 'The Resurrection of the Soul by Grace' and then he commented:

Look up to God, anticipating the Resurrection! The earth is a wilderness, but it is the land of Judah, if God's Praise hallows our hopes. Faith anticipates the blessing. The Church militant must praise God, looking to drink of His Divine fulness. We thirst because we drink. The thirst is the very measure of our life, and not to thirst is to die. There is no water upon earth to refresh the soul. The only water of refreshment comes from the throne of God. It is the very Blood of the Lamb spiritually communicated from the glorified Body of the Crucified.[42]

This 63rd Psalm has, according to Chrysostom, been the morning song of the Church from early times, and Benedict placed it daily in the office of Lauds. Yet Fr. Benson insisted that these psalms should be brought out of the monastic choir into the rough and tumble of life.

We should accustom ourselves to this practical familiarity with the Psalter, bringing it in so as to meet the wants of daily life, finding in the wants of daily life a real opportunity of sympathy with our Lord Jesus Christ . . . . If we are to do this it must be in the power of the Holy Spirit. The same Spirit by which David beforehand was inspired to write the words is necessary for us, if we are to speak them.[43]

Yet it was with the daily divine office that Fr. Benson particularly linked this typological interpretation—but equally with Christ's dwelling in us through the sacraments.

Our worship springs out of our union with Christ, that it is, so to speak, the flowering of our Eucharist . . . . Our Baptismal life, by which we are really and truly incorporated into Christ, and our Eucharistic life, by which that Baptismal life is nourished, rise up into the sublime dignity of our daily office—the Psalter, the anthology of God, the blossoming of the divine glory.[44]

Through this use of the Psalter we realize our unity with the whole Church here and beyond death.

What multitudes have been perfected in the life of Christ, while these words of power filled their hearts, rose from their lips, ruled their lives, checked their fears, deepened their penitence, stimulated their hopes, formulated their thanksgivings.[45]

This has of course been the traditional practice of the Church; and is still commended in our days by, for example, Thomas Merton, who writes of those

who *know by experience* that the Psalms are a perfect prayer, a prayer in which Christ prays in the Christian soul uniting that soul to the Father in himself. They have entered into the Psalms with faith. They have in a sense 'lived' out the meaning of some of the Psalms in their own lives.[46]

Yet for Fr. Benson this typological interpretation was not just a 'devotional device' to give more meaning to the divine office and prayer. This interpretation was rather the inspiration of his whole life and ministry. Fr. Powell of his Society, who had known him during his years in the United States, visited him in Oxford in 1900. Fr. Benson was now seventy-six, very feeble on his legs and nearly blind. Fr. Powell went with him and heard him preach at St. Barnabas Church. He wrote his impression:

He preached on the *Psalter* with amazing force for something over a full hour. I never heard him preach like that in America—indeed never have I heard *Christ* preached as he was that evening.[47]

This way of handling the Psalter does not commend itself to many scholars today, but it did very much to so influential a theologian as Dietrich Bonhoeffer. He said to his war-time students in the German Confessing Church:

The Psalter is the vicarious prayer of Christ for his Church . . . . Only in the whole Christ does the whole Psalter become a reality, a whole which the individual can never fully comprehend and call his own.[48]

His friend Eberhard Bethge said how eager Bonhoeffer was to possess Fr. Benson's *Way of Holiness*, because, as he said,

He had learnt at the university that this Psalm 119 was the most boring of the Psalms; but now he regarded its interpretation as the climax of his theological life.[49]

HISTORICAL BIBLICAL STUDY

Fr. Benson was never able to grasp that discriminating modern historical study can deepen our love of the Bible and our spiritual profit from it. This is strange, because he was no blind obscurantist. He urged on his community, as we have seen, an arduous study of the languages and of the exact text of scripture. He himself was ready to question authorities whom he respected; for example, he admitted even of the Fathers, 'We have frequently to see how they erred through want of knowledge in their day which we now possess.'[50] He also had at least an amateur interest in the progress of science: 'We have in this century to keep in touch with scientific discovery.'[51]

This scientific method of investigation was applied, particularly in Germany, first to classical history and then to biblical history. Some of these German critics proceeded to very negative conclusions—due largely to their philosophical presuppositions—much to the alarm of Pusey and Benson. But the hands of the clock cannot stand still. The answer to these critics would seem to be an equally painstaking research on sounder presuppositions. This was taking place in England during Benson's lifetime; for example, through Bishop Lightfoot's commentaries on the Pauline Epistles, starting in 1865, and through his book, *Essays on Supernatural Religion* in 1889, itself a devastating reply to a radical theory from Tübingen, which treated many of the New Testament books as unreliable documents of the second century.

But to Fr. Benson any acceptance, however small, of biblical criticism—whatever the motive—was compromise with, even if not betrayal to, unbelief. He particularly opposed *Lux Mundi*, a collection of essays of liberal Catholic scholars, published in 1889. He called it worldly light, *Lux Mundana*[52] and is said to have refused to meet any of these scholars.[53] Bishop Gore himself in a revised preface to its tenth edition in 1890 made it clear that he followed only the more moderate critics and not the extreme and frankly rationalist ones. He said explicitly that he aimed not at a 'compromise', but at a 'correlation' of the Church's faith with painstaking work of biblical scholars, and that the critical positions, which he himself accepted, were 'compatible with the real *inspiration* of the Old Testament'.

Fr. Benson would have none of it, although he spoke out against an unfair attack on the book, adding typically:

Controversy is very apt to have the effect of boiling water upon tea-leaves, in bringing out what is poisonous after it has brought out what is refreshing.[54]

Yet in old age he could sometimes write querulously:

The devotional books will not sell unless there is a tinge of compromise with unbelief—otherwise they have no chance of being circulated. They are simply ignored.[55]

But near the very end of Fr. Benson's life, Bishop Gore, who greatly admired him, called to give him his blessing. And when the bishop asked for a special day of prayer and fasting during the 1914–18 war, Fr. Benson forgave him all his liberalism.

We owe an immense debt to Fr. Benson for laying so profound a foundation of biblical spirituality for his Society and for all whom he influenced. There is need today of biblical spirituality—on rather different presuppositions—for there are methods of meditation now being taught which bypass the Bible. Fr. Benson himself would, I am sure, call us to practise and teach biblical spirituality—and to find out *how* to do this now. He required of each of his followers to be ready for the tasks of his own day.

This makes the religious to be specially a man—not simply of the day, but a man of the moment, a man precisely up to the mark of the times. This makes the religious—so far from being the traditional imitator of by-gone days,—most especially a man of the present moment and its life. His duties throw him into the interests of the present moment . . . . The religious therefore reviews calmly, dispassionately, dutifully, all the phenomena of the age in which he lives. He does not review them as things to deplore, but as things to rejoice in, and as things to be acted upon.[56]

5
Father Benson: Man of Prayer—
Some Critical Reflections

C. R. Bryant SSJE

THE MAN

SOME forty years after Fr. Benson's death I remember Fr. Strong,
an old man then, telling me that he had been infirmarian during
the father's last years. Often he had occasion to go into Fr.
Benson's cell and frequently he found him on his knees praying,
totally oblivious of his entrance. When alone he used to pray
aloud, each word uttered with intense meaning; he would say the
Lord's prayer like that, passionately intent on God. In Fr.
Strong's words, 'he was there', in the heavenly places, hidden
with Christ in God, dead to everything else. It was this sure
contact with heavenly reality which impressed those who were at
all spiritually sensitive when they met Fr. Benson. In 1920 Dr
Edward Faulkner, then organist of Bombay Cathedral, recalled
the impression Fr. Benson made on a brief stay during 1891 in a
large house in Allahabad where he himself had been residing at
the time.

Father Benson's influence in the house was extraordinary. When he had
been living in the house for a week or so my servants, who could not
speak English at all, came to me and said 'What kind of Holy Man is this
that has come to stay in the house? He never sleeps, but prays far into the
hours of the night. He truly is a man of God.' When he left the house all
the servants, Moslem and Hindu, lined up and made a profound saluta-
tion to him.[1]

People were struck by him as transparently a man who spoke of
God out of direct experience. Bishop Gore commented on this
quality of genuineness in the sermon he preached to commem-
orate the centenary of Fr. Benson's birth. 'Three times', he said, 'I
happened to hear men use about him an almost identical expression. Once it was a vigorous business man, twice it was young

75

priests, all of them having been in retreats conducted by Fr. Benson, and having been overwhelmed by the impressiveness of his message. They all said at different times: "Well, after all, that is the real thing." That is what you felt in his presence, "That is the real thing".'[2]

It is to be noted that the three whom Bishop Gore quotes had all been in a retreat conducted by him. Canon Allchin in his introductory essay calls attention to Fr. Benson's extraordinary power as a retreat conductor. In that role he seemed more at home than at any other time. He spoke without notes, without apparent preparation, as though by inspiration. In a memoir contributed after his death to the *Church Times* Fr. Maturin writes of the retreats he conducted in the chapel of the old mission house:

I heard many of his addresses in that chapel, spread over a period of many years, and for fertility and originality of thought and the abundant gift of expression and illustration I have never heard his equal.[3]

It seems that when conducting retreats he received a special gift of the Holy Spirit for opening the things of God to his hearers. For he was not a popular preacher and was both in matter and manner above the heads of the congregation of an ordinary parish church.

Fr. Benson gave his contemporaries the impression of a man speaking from the heart a present spiritual reality of which he was powerfully conscious. It seems that he was a contemplative, familiar from experience with the darkness of passive contemplation and of the emptiness of mind which sometimes accompanies strong aspirations of the heart towards God. But at the same time he had learnt to combine the contemplative intuition of God with thinking and theologizing. This is a rare gift, for contemplation which is a predominantly passive attitude, a listening, a waiting, a looking towards God in loving trust, cannot readily be combined with active concentrated thinking. Indeed it is normal for those who are drawn to this intuitive approach to God to be totally unable to combine it with controlled thinking. This ability to combine two apparently contradictory mental attitudes was partly due, no doubt, to an unusually vigorous intelligence to which both his contemporaries and his writings bear witness. But it must also have been in part the reward of years of discipline and prayer.

It is possible that he overdid the self-restraint of those years of preparation. Fr. Maturin speaks of his limitations, of 'his shyness and reserve intensified by his theory of detachment'. He records the remark Fr. Benson made to him 'I never knew anyone intimately'. His Oxford friend and contemporary, H. P. Liddon, the well-known preacher and Canon of St. Paul's, spoke of his 'odd severity'. But before we judge him by standards appropriate to more ordinary men or to our own age, we should ask the question whether, being the man he was and living when he did, he could have acted otherwise without renouncing his vocation. For he was a man aflame with the desire to be at one with God, whom he loved, trusted and wanted to serve. This was for him the pearl of great price, for the sake of which he counted the world well lost. The treasure on which his heart was set was no distant goal merely but a present possession, the realized union with God, which effectively robbed renunciation of the note of sadness or weariness. He was a man of immense energy, a fighter, whose native aggression though held in tight rein was sometimes in evidence. The title which he gave to his devotional commentary on the Psalms, *The War Songs of the Prince of Peace,* suggests an element in his own temperament. He was a war horse whose heart lifted at the scent of battle. His sardonic humour, his contemptuous refusal of any softness or self-indulgence, his admiration for the martyr's fortitude, all tell us something of the battle he fought to subdue his instincts into obedience to the heavenly vision. This personal battle of a man of strong passions may go some way towards explaining an element of exaggeration in his antagonism to worldly society and rebelliousness of the flesh.

HIS SPIRITUAL TEACHING

Before turning to the content of Fr. Benson's spiritual teaching something must be said about its biblical roots and his way of using the great scriptural symbols. Another essay has written of his dependence on the Bible for inspiration and his typological method of interpreting the scriptures. Further light is shed on his thinking by a theologian who was born when Fr. Benson was over eighty, became an associate of his Society and must have been well acquainted with his writings, Austin Farrer. Farrer reflected deeply on what might be called the psychology of inspiration and what he has written about the inspiration of the apostolic writers illuminates the way Fr. Benson's mind worked when he spoke or wrote about God. In Farrer's view the Apostles' understanding of Christ derives from Christ's own understanding of his person and mission in terms of and in fulfilment of great Old Testament images, such as those of God's enthroned majesty ruling all things, of the Adam, the man spoken of in Daniel, of the patriarch Israel with his twelve sons, of David the anointed king, of the suffering servant of Isaiah, of covenant, of sacrifice, of communion. These images were interpreted by Jesus in the light of his union with the Father and of the course events took as he followed his inspiration. In the minds of the apostolic writers, according to Farrer, 'the great images interpreted the events of Christ's ministry, death and resurrection and the events interpreted the images; the interplay of the two is revelation'.[4] Again Farrer writes 'The stuff of inspiration is living images.'[5] To understand scripture 'we have to listen to the Spirit speaking divine things and the way to appreciate his speech is to quicken our own minds with the life of the inspired images.'[6] Whether or not Farrer has understood apostolic inspiration I think he sheds much light on the way in which Fr. Benson spoke and wrote. The images lived again in his mind, focusing his imagination upon the living Christ of whom they spoke, and releasing the inspiration and energy with which he communicated his vision. I think this explains the profoundly biblical character of his retreat addresses, given without a note, with perfect fluency and without apparently any special preparation.

The central focus of Fr. Benson's spiritual teaching was Christ, risen and glorified, reigning in heaven, and, through the Holy Spirit, dwelling in the individual Christian. He used spatial metaphors freely but was not taken in by them; he constantly spoke of looking up to Christ in glory, but this was in no way inconsistent with turning to the glorified Christ within.

The real knowledge of the truth is that joyous knowledge which we can only have when we look up and see Christ, or rather when we look inward and see Christ. To us upward means inward: for the higher world is that glorified existence of the Great Mediator who stands to us in the relation, not of an apex to a triangle, but of a central point of power to the solid sphere which feels its motions, Himself 'unmoved all motion's Source' — by creative power in the outer world, by mediatorial grace in the sphere of supernatural life. People have so little notion of the real Presence of

Christ within them as the basis of all sanctity, just as the personal Presence of the Spirit of Christ is the active principle of all sanctity.[7]

The presence of the indwelling Christ, which he understood dynamically as an active influence, was utterly real to Fr. Benson. It may well have been partly this that led him to exalt the sacrament of baptism which initiated this indwelling. Blindness to the presence of Christ within them led people to a distorted view of the Eucharist.

In Western Christendom the Holy Eucharist has so entirely overshadowed Holy Baptism, that the food of our life is made to be a gift greater than the life which it sustains. Without a full acknowledgment of the supernatural change wrought at our baptism our spiritual life becomes a metaphor.[8]

This stress on the greatness of baptism in no way implied a low view of the Eucharist:

. . . it is for the purpose of cementing, stablishing, perfecting, developing this union [sc. with Christ] that we come to the Blessed Sacrament, and each communion must be a fresh binding of ourselves in body, soul, and spirit to the glorious being of the risen Son of God.[9]

In Holy Eucharist we go within the veil, and receive from Him that which is His. He communicates to us that which we need. His Body is the Ark of the Covenant, and while we feed thereon we receive from Him the treasure of grace which He has in Himself and which He distributes to us in proportion as we ask for it.[10]

The indwelling of Christ, risen and glorified, within the Christian is, I believe, an important key to the spirituality of Fr. Benson. But to say this could be to invite misunderstanding at a time when Jesus cults have arisen which express an untheological devotion to Jesus as a great and inspiring teacher and leader, and when some theologians understand the Incarnation as only a notable instance of God's indwelling in every man. His theology is through and through Trinitarian. Christ is the Word made flesh. To speak of the indwelling of Christ is to imply the indwelling of the blessed Trinity. In Christ God shews us a human face, touches us with human hands, loves us with a human heart. The sacrament of baptism which initiates us into the life of Christ takes us into the life of the Godhead; it makes us sons in the Son; it brings us to share in the giving and receiving of the blessed Trinity. The centrality of the doctrine of the triune

Godhead in the teaching of Fr. Benson is abundantly illustrated in Martin Smith's chapter on his theological vision.

He uses a number of images in order to make real the presence of Christ within the Christian. One of these is that of light, more especially the sun. The risen Christ is the sun that creates the day in which the Christian lives.

The Sun of righteousness fills the sky of the soul, and the stars of the night season are lost to sight. If they from time to time shine out, it is because the Sun is suffering eclipse. The only way to get rid of those stars is by hastening to walk in the light of the Lord. The Sun of righteousness suffers eclipse in our souls, not by reason of external obstacles but by the failure of faith, hope and charity, whereby we ought to abide in His light.[11]

He speaks of the Christian as a ray of the sun's light.

We are as His rays, and a ray cannot be taken away from the sun. It lives by a perpetual energy of that light which is the source of all other rays; and all are one in their source, their life, their spreading power.[12]

The presence of Christ is the sun which both lights up the heavenly Jerusalem and illumines the Christian inwardly:

. . . this light is not a mere external light, as the Pillar of fire, illuminating the surface of things round about us; . . . rather, it is an inward light filling our souls, and enabling us, as it were, to see in the dark. The darkness remains externally round about us, the darkness of the world, but the soul which is living in the light of the heavenly Jerusalem sees by reason of the light of the inner presence of Jesus Christ.[13]

Another powerful image of Christ which he uses is that of the voice of God. The idea is a natural extension from the meaning of the Word of God. After speaking of the call of Abraham he writes: 'That Voice (sc. which called Abraham) has become flesh.'[14] The voice is creative and invigorating. 'This Voice is the inspiring principle of fortitude. We have a vigour, a courage, a power that is more than our own.'[15] He speaks of the presence of the Voice of God in anyone who has received a special call from God to a way of life, which he interprets broadly not only as the religious life in the technical sense but any way of life followed in response to God's call.

The Voice of God is the revelation of the Word of God within the soul, and we must reverence this presence even through the infirmities of the outer vessel. Every soul that has received such a call must be reverenced, as possessing a special presence. Whether it is true or untrue to its vocation matters not; the presence is there, if there has been the vocation.[16]

An illustration of the importance for him of the image of the voice is his use in most of the meditations of *The Final Passover* of an imagined dialogue in which the Christian addresses Christ and Christ speaks in response. One of the ways in which the Christian becomes aware of Christ is as a voice addressing his conscience.

Of equal importance with Christ's indwelling, in the teaching of Fr. Benson, is that of the indwelling of the Holy Spirit. He took for granted the truth implicit in the unity of the triune Godhead that each of the Persons of the Trinity is present in the action of the others, so that for example it is possible to ascribe the grace of God either to the action of Christ or to that of the Spirit, or indeed to that of the Father. But he understands Christ as especially the illuminator of man's conscience, 'which is the mediatorial channel of our nature, and it is through this channel that the waters of illuminating grace must flow'.[17] The Holy Ghost, however, 'dwells not in the conscience itself but in the affections. The Holy Ghost is the Spirit of love, as the Son of God is the power and wisdom of God—the power of truth.'[18] Unless our hearts and affections are moved by the Spirit we are powerless to obey the Voice of Christ.

The Spirit speaking in our hearts gives power and efficacy to the voice of conscience. This Spirit makes the glory of Christ to shine within us. This Spirit makes the conscience to ring with the unutterable power of the Word of God.[19]

In the thought of Fr. Benson the teaching of Holy Scripture, illuminated by that of the early Fathers, is reinterpreted in the light of his own immediate experience of the things of God. He does not use the language of dynamic psychology nor speak of the unconscious, but he knows that the renewal of our being cannot come about by any effort of will or intelligence, it can only result from life and energy flooding up from within. This renewal from the depths of our being is the work of the Holy Ghost.

If we enter into ourselves we shall find the ground of our heart as it were broken up, and a deep well springing up from beneath it. There we find admission into the Being of God . . . Our life is hidden in God and yet continually manifesting itself as from God; hidden in God, yet continually rising up into manifestations of blessed intercourse with God. The life to which we retire in the contemplation of God makes itself manifest as a well of Living Water. This well springs up from within us in no bubbling, spasmodic manner; it is continual, imperceptible, the mighty power of God rising up through our littleness—expanding our nature—gradually overflowing it—until our nature is lost to sight.[20]

True repentance, the change of attitude by which a person's whole life becomes oriented towards God, can only come about through the action of God in the depths of his being.

When the Holy Ghost really works in us our sins begin to be done away, the consequences of our sins begin to leave us. As the frost binds up the waters, and the frosts being loosened the streams immediately begin to flow; so when the soul is delivered from the frost of sin, when the heat of the Holy Ghost penetrates, then the soul finds movements of holy contrition that circulate through all its faculties.[21]

Our contrition is the melting of our whole being, and the filling of our whole being with a joyous consciousness of Divine love.[22]

The contrite heart which opens a person to God's compassion is not the effect of trying to make ourselves feel sorry.

Contrition is not an operation of the soul but an operation of the Holy Ghost in the soul, which loosens its hardness and takes the soul out of itself into entire self-surrender.[23]

Baptism which incorporates us into the Spirit-filled body of Christ initiates this indwelling of the Holy Spirit.

The Spirit does not fall upon us from without, but from within. As we are the members of Christ's Body, the Spirit of Christ comes to us by that interior organization of His Body whereby our souls possess their vital union with Him. The full gift of the Spirit is communicated to us in Holy Baptism, but the gift then received is developed by fresh communications of strength from Christ, the Head.[24]

Fr. Benson understands a genuine Christian life as one lived as much as possible in the consciousness of and reliance upon this indwelling Spirit. It is not enough to turn to him in times of emergency.

The Holy Ghost manifests His indwelling on special occasions oy various gifts, but His presence is not intermittent. If we would have the Holy Ghost with us on certain occasions of special need, we must be continually attentive to His presence, giving Him constant homage. We are said to be full of the Holy Ghost if all our actions are done in His power. Our actions are the development of ourselves, and if the Holy Ghost dwells with us we must be careful that all our acts are done with His cooperation. Then He will fill those actions, and they become to us the means of continual renewal and power.[25]

The fortitude which is of the Holy Ghost is a principle of strength to all around; it breathes an atmosphere of invigorating love. Though a manifestation of individual strength, yet it is felt to be a pillar of strength to all around.[26]

We continually forget to rely on this indwelling power; our difficulties and trials by driving us to rely on the Spirit are opportunities of growing in union with God.

In all our temptations we must choose to dwell in God by the power of the Holy Ghost. This is one part of the value of our life of temptation. It forces us to exercise the gift of the Holy Ghost as the inspiring principle of our will; and by this act of choice we abide in God, and become partakers of His glory.[27]

Four emphases in Fr. Benson's teaching about prayer need to be noted: it is through and through Trinitarian; it stresses the importance of Bible-inspired meditation as a preparation for prayer; this meditation should lead to a prayer of the heart, to praise and adoration, and to contemplation; finally he places great emphasis on intercession for others. First he understands Christian prayer as a participation in the 'circulating life of the Trinity', as the individualizing of the prayer of Christ to the Father through the Spirit. In so far as our prayer is genuine it is Christ's own prayer offered through us in the power of the Spirit. Writing of prayer for others he says:

Our prayers are but the individualizing of the prayer of Christ, who is the Head of the whole body; and our acts of penitence are merely forms of prayer through which He still pleads with the Father by the power of the Holy Ghost. If our acts are to avail for others, they must also avail to make us more closely united to Christ. If they do the one they do the other.[28]

But prayer is very especially the work of the Spirit in us. Expanding the teaching of St. Paul in the eighth chapter of the Epistle to the Romans he writes:

It is the Holy Ghost Who must also help us in our prayers—or, more truly, He must pray in us with groanings which our nature cannot utter. The voice of the Spirit rises to the ear of the Father. Too often we choke that utterance by our own earthliness, wanting to take some part in the work to ourselves. We do most when we leave Him to do all. Our words simply supply the form of His utterance. The power is ever His. We should endeavour to realize how lovingly and personally He pleads within us . . . The sense of repose in making our own worship subsidiary in all respects to His inspirations will save us from much exhaustion, disquiet, distraction, despondency.[29]

Again, 'Consider the Holy Ghost as dwelling within thy heart, and rising up from thy heart as a flame burning towards heaven.'[30]

As a preparation for prayer Fr. Benson sets great store by meditation on the scriptures. The six books of *The Final Passover* as well as *Benedictus Dominus* were designed to provide help for this biblical gateway into prayer.

By the Sacraments God takes hold upon us, and works invisibly in us. By meditation we take hold upon His invisible presence, feed upon Him in our souls, receive the illumination of His Holy Spirit, grow in grace and become perfectly united to Him.[31]

In meditating on the scriptures he expects us to grasp the invisible Christ of whom the scriptures speak. This is partly a work of imagination, but an imagination controlled by the creed. 'It is not enough that we read of what God reveals. We must have His truth revealed to ourselves and that can only be by His Spirit.'[32] Meditation as he envisaged it was much more an exercise of the heart and the affections than of the head; it was reflection with a view to communing with God; it aimed at leading a person to a loving knowledge of God through the Holy Spirit. He saw it as an opening of ourselves to some divine truth as a means to deepening divine love.

We do not come to meditation merely that we may see, but that we may learn to gaze in holy love. So we must rest upon the point until the loving affection of our heart is really drawn towards it by the inspiration of the Holy Ghost. We must speak with the Holy Ghost respecting it, consult as it were with the blessed Spirit dwelling in our hearts, and ask Him to teach us how we may best love this manifestation of divine truth.[33]

He understood the regular practice of meditation as a powerful means to a life in which habitual interior prayer is both the companion and the inspiration. 'Prayer, this interior prayer, is the very act by which the soul lives. It is the movement of the Spirit of God within the soul.'[34] It will be seen that the place of the reasoning intellect in Fr. Benson's teaching is real but subordinate. He would have been critical of those modern schools of meditation which try to bypass reason altogether. Meditation and the movement of the heart lead on to the prayer of contemplative waiting upon God, of looking and loving.

Contemplation is the highest and hardest work. You must be content to lie still in God's hands, and leave Him to do everything.[35]

Again,

We must be content simply to live in the hands of God, without dictation, and without desire. The soul must wait in stillness upon God, with the simple infantine gaze of loving confidence. 'Of Him cometh my salvation.' 'He that shall come will come.' We must not think to hasten His coming except by the stillness of our expectant homage. He cannot come to us unless we are simply satisfied to let Him do all He wills, and when He wills.[36]

In darkness and unknowing the soul apprehends God in love.

We must meet the agnosticism of the present day, which rejoices in putting God aside, with that true agnosticism which rejoices in simple absorbing love. But although love confesses its ignorance, it delights to approach towards that which it shall know hereafter. And our reasonings are not to satisfy the insults of unbelief, but the cravings of sweet desire. The dazzling glow of the divine life prevents our seeing things in God—seeing God as He is; but we can see forms in our own nature, mind and heart, created as we are in His image, which serve to lead us onward to worship Him in truth and praise Him with a humble prostration of the intelligence.[37]

He writes of the fear of the darkness, of the unknown, and of the faith which enables the Christian to pass through it.

So we are often fearful and cast down as we enter into the darkness—the cloud preparing for a transfiguration glory. We must not be worried if we find it is so, for, in fact, this is the very necessity of the darkness. A darkness which was not felt would be no real darkness. The soul must pass through its own darkness . . . and this is the victory by which we pass securely through the darkness, even our faith.[38]

This waiting on God should give a security to the Christian at all times and in all his actions.

This rest remains. It is not merely future. We are to experience it now. We must act in its strength, the peace of God which passeth all understanding. It is the possession of this sure abiding place which gives us stability amidst a changing world; and this home with Jesus is a place of repose for us, so that we can be detached from place and associations of every earthly home.[39]

The fourth characteristic emphasis in Fr. Benson's teaching about prayer is on intercession. He founded a confraternity for intercessory prayer whose members undertook to spend a quarter of an hour daily in intercession for others, and he published a *Manual of Intercessory Prayer* to help the members. He regarded it as a safeguard against two great dangers of private prayer— formality on the one hand and dreaminess on the other.

We shall probably realise the Divine power more fully, and so we shall hold better communion with God, if we have definite objects of prayer external to ourselves, than if we merely spend our time in aspirations after a holy life. We must avoid selfishness even in praying for ourselves. There may be a mere dreamy desire of our own good without effort at improvement. Nothing will benefit ourselves or correct selfishness more than an earnest habit of intercession for the spiritual advancement of others.[40]

Of course, Fr. Benson sees intercession as a more than human work. It is a sharing in the intercession of Christ.

We are not to think of Christ's supplication on our behalf as that of an external Intercessor. He intercedes for us by communicating to us the glory of His own exalted life. He does not intercede as one separate from those for whom He intercedes, but they are, as it were, so many mouths to Himself; and as they pray for themselves His voice fills their utterance with the authority and claim belonging to Himself.[41]

Intercession is further an expression of love and a means through which love grows and spreads through the world; it is therefore a work of the Holy Spirit.

Prayer is the great energy of love and this prayer is the voice of the Holy Ghost. We cannot intercede for one another simply in the strength of our old nature. We need the power of the Holy Ghost. It is the Holy Ghost who must enable us to sympathize, to feel so truly the needs of others as to pray for them properly . . . the Holy Ghost takes us out of ourselves that we may lose ourselves in those for whom we pray and pray for them in the simple interest of their own persons; or rather the Holy Ghost so identifies us with those for whom we pray, that we come to realise Christ in them, and it is the divine life, the divine glory in them, which is the object of our intercession.[42]

The Christian's whole life should be intercessory and part of the value of specific intercessory prayer is to give an intercessory intention to the rest of life. 'If, instead of talking to people as much as we do, we would pray for them how much more would be accomplished.'[43] At the same time intercession though reaching up to heaven rises out of the actual circumstances and needs of others.

Intercession takes its stand on the reality of the world as God has formed it, as Satan has marred it, and as man has misused it; and if our intercessions are to be really valuable they must be grounded on the actual facts of this world's experience.[44]

There are two further emphases in Fr. Benson's spiritual doctrine which must be considered before it will be possible to form some critical estimate of his spirituality as a whole. It was directed towards the future and looked confidently to heaven as the goal of the Christian life; and it was a life of conflict, presupposing and demanding a radical break with the world, a kind of death.

The Christian's hope is set on a supernatural destiny, sometimes thought of as the return of Christ to establish the reign of God, which Fr. Benson looked forward to keenly and believed might well occur in his lifetime, sometimes as a life in heaven lived in union with Christ and in fellowship with all the redeemed. This unblushing hope of heaven will seem scandalous to some modern Christians who, in Austin Farrer's words

profess the Christian name and nevertheless are ashamed of heavenly hope. The cry is raised 'a this-worldly religion. There may be a bonus hereafter—only better not count on it.' But I tell you that Christianity cannot for any length of time survive the amputation of such a limb as life to come.[45]

Fr. Benson would have wholeheartedly agreed with Farrer's affirmation. He was well aware of the corruption of heavenly hope either into that of the satisfaction of selfish desire or into the neglect of the duties of the present.

Heaven must not be looked forward to as the mere gratification of our desires, but as the joy of God in the perfection of our being.[46]

The hope of heaven frees the Christian from undue anxiety about the future as well as from clinging to the past either in nostalgia or resentment.

The really detached man is living with all his energy summed up in the present moment. He is able to take up with everything just as God presents it to him. He is not on the lookout for things at a distance, but what comes within the immediate area of contemplation. He is always looking round about him to see what there is in sight, but never troubles about what has passed away, nor is he fidgeted by what may possibly come next. The present moment becomes a moment of intense reality to the ready man.[47]

The glory of heaven to which the Christian looks forward will not be something extraneous to him; it will not be something totally discontinuous with the past. 'The glory which shall be our joy there is the very same that has been our strength here. It is not the earning of a future reward but the revealing of a present strength.'[48] The life of heaven is the growth into full blossom of a relationship to God through Christ which has been begun here.

The full flowering of this relationship belongs to the other side of the grave. The discontinuity of death is the necessary gateway to the heavenly life of total union with God. Similarly a kind of death precedes the beginning of our life in Christ and accompanies its growth. The seed of this death is sown in baptism which symbolizes it. But what is there set forth in symbol must be realized in practice by a death to all that is resistant to the Kingdom, all that contradicts the sovereignty of Christ or thwarts the action of the Holy Spirit. This practical realization of the meaning of baptismal union with Christ involves the Christian in battle and demands a fighting faith, courage and endurance. Fr. Benson sees this conflict in the stark and simple terms of a fight to the death with Satan, the great deceiver and prince of this world. Indeed he can depict the Christian life as one of prayer and conflict. 'It is the contemplative life gazing up to God and doing battle with Satan, which is the essential characteristic of all Christian life.'[49] The more dedicated a Christian is to God and his Kingdom the fiercer will be the battle with the Adversary.

If we give ourselves to God, we may be quite sure that Satan will not suffer us to be simply withdrawn from his power without having the reality of our self-oblation fully proved.[50]

The Christian life is not peace but war.

There can be no rest except in proportion to the struggle, no vision except in proportion to the purification of heart, no purification except in proportion as the agony of Satanic conflict squeezes out the life-blood of our corrupt nature.[51]

The most characteristic experience of the conflict with Satan is the absence of the consciousness of God, which Fr. Benson sees as nothing else than the presence of the Enemy. The only way to overcome is total trust in God, 'we must trust and not despair'.

This conflict with Satan is itself a kind of dying. Physical death is essentially passive, it is something that happens to a person; in it he is forced to relinquish his possessions, to lose control of his bodily being, to let go of physical life. The spiritual dying which is the door into the new life in Christ involves the resolute and determined letting go of whatever hinders that new life. But though the letting go of the old logically precedes the laying hold of the new in practice they are simultaneous. It is only as we grasp the new that we are able to let go of the old. So death to the old habits and attitudes begins to occur as we grow in faith, hope and charity. Mortification in the active sense, fasting, the renunciation of particular pleasures, the undertaking of disagreeable tasks, seeks to assist the passive letting go of selfish ways and so to cooperate with the life-giving Spirit.

We die to ourselves, not merely by the negative efforts of natural morality, but by the positive energies of faith working by love.[52]

Active mortification is of use in so far as it deepens our union with Christ.

External mortifications are valuable, not so much because they punish or purify the material nature by any inherent power, although this is one of their subordinate uses, but chiefly because in practising them we are calling into energy the mind of Christ, and are identifying ourselves with His Passion as an active law of sympathy.[53]

This spiritual dying is a letting go of selfish inclinations, a deliberate saying no to the tendency to cling to pleasure or some object of ambition. It is the indispensable precondition of bringing Christian life to others.

We cannot give forth life save by dying. Many a mortification of the outer nature is needed, not mere austerity, for that does not always mortify, but a real dying to ourselves. 'I die daily' is the law of apostolic life . . . Any disappointments we have had are often much more resultful in blessings for the future than success would have been.[54]

The pattern of this spiritual letting go is Christ's death on the cross and Fr. Benson understands it as a sharing in Christ's crucifixion.

We must be living true to the Crucified. We cannot overleap that step in evangelical life. It is not enough for us to point to Him; He must be manifest in us, still crucified in the world, though glorified in the world beyond. Such a number are carried away with the dream that, as Christ has died, we may live in this world as the results of His triumph. It is like claiming to take possession of an enemy's capital by lodging in a hovel on some battlefield of victory. This world can never be to us anything but a hovel and a battlefield. The country we claim is on the other side of the dark river. The less we have to make ourselves feel at home here the better. The most dangerous times are when all things are smooth.[55]

Sickness and physical suffering can bring much blessing:

. . . bodily suffering is one of the best ways of rising up to Him, and we become fitted to speak of the transfiguring life just in proportion as we have been taken into the cloud. In so many ways the day of the Lord is darkness and not light. It is darkness which prepares us, darkness which preserves us, darkness which perfects us. Illuminations are very un-trustworthy. If we have eyes to see the darkness, it is much better for us. Light cometh in the 'morning' and darkness may be of bodily weakness, of outward suffering and necessity of body, or spiritual temptation, or absence of comfort and joy and divine consciousness.[56]

SOME CRITICAL REFLECTIONS

The spirit of energetic antagonism to Satan and the world which fills Fr. Benson's writings was by no means congenial to the second half of the nineteenth century. In the theological form in which this hostility is expressed it is hardly congenial to the second half of the twentieth, but it is possible now to appreciate its profound insight. The destruction of two world wars and the cruelty and mass murder of Belsen and Auschwitz have destroyed what illusions we may have cherished about man's natural goodness. They have also made it easier to believe in a trans-personal evil over and above the personal evil which each indivi-dual needs to resist. Dynamic psychology sees this latter as the shadow cast by a person's conscious aims and ideals, the elements of his personality, such as his aggression, his fear, his sex drive, which he has partly rejected or not allowed to develop, which in their repressed condition interfere with and frustrate his con-scious intentions. A person grows to maturity as he learns to accept these rejected elements and manage them responsibly and by so doing dissolves or at least much diminishes the interfering shadow. But there is an archetypal evil, a collective tendency to arrogance and brutality, a racial shadow, which cannot like the personal shadow be assimilated. It must be recognized, confronted and resisted, or it will tend to dominate the individual without his realizing it. The existence of trans-personal evil has led some contemporary writers to make use of the category of the demonic to describe it. The demonic is not only manifested in spectacular evils such as genocide or the cruelties of the concentration camp or the use of torture, but in the unacceptable faces of capitalism and communism, and the comfortable blindness of well-meaning people to the injustice and inhumanity from which they profit. The demonic is expressed in an atmosphere which blunts the moral sensibility and makes crass selfishness look like reasonable prudence. All this evil is for Fr. Benson personified as Satan, as an Enemy to be fought, as a deceiver to be unmasked, as a spiritual atmosphere to be resisted. If we wish to demythologize Satan let us take care not to underestimate the demonic and weaken our capacity to fight it.

The prominent place given in Fr. Benson's teaching to the spiritual conflict may give it the appearance of one-sidedness. But his whole life was a protest on behalf of truths about God which he saw to be half-forgotten, a protest against an emasculated Christianity. Yet if he stresses one particular side of the gospel he was aware of the other side though he seldom alludes to it. Bishop Gore in a sermon already referred to described an occasion when at a gathering in an Oxford senior common room Fr. Benson in a memorable and impressive speech had seemed to suggest that there was no other way of living the Christian life than through the outward and visible renunciation of the religious life.

An old-fashioned and much-respected tutor, Mr Woollcombe, rose and, in words which I very well remember, uttered a protest in favour of the life of the good man living in the world, and the life of marriage and the Christian family, as being a true following of Christ. Fr. Benson did not explain himself; he simply rose at the end of the protest and said: 'I hope I hardly need to say that I cordially agree with everything that Mr Woollcombe has said'.[57]

Fr. Benson says much against 'the world' and the worldly spirit but he can appreciate the beauty of the Taj Mahal, the splendour of Niagara and the many Christian qualities of people immersed in the secular world. Addressing religious who have renounced the world he says:

The world is a glorious world: it is a world which has its own value. It is formed of God for great and noble purposes. It is not because the eye is blind to the capacities of the world that we are to turn aside from it, but because the eye has been opened by the power of faith to behold greater realities.[58]

He sometimes uses violent images in describing the Christian's warfare. He speaks of the necessity of having our affections crushed, but it is in order that they may be renewed and purified.

The affections need indeed to be crushed, in order that they may spring up and be given to God. God does not crush out the affections by simply cutting down the tree. God prunes, and, as He prunes, enables the tree to grow with a better growth. He cuts down in order that He may graft in, and He would let the old life grow with new fruitfulness. And so He calls us into religion to have our affections crushed, but developed. Our old affections were mere selfishness. Our new affections spring from and return to God, as their proper centre. Our affections rested upon earthly things, earthly friends; now they live in God, and all are loved in accordance with the will of God, and for the glory of God.[59]

It is to be noted that these words are addressed to religious, and a great deal of his writings similarly have religious in mind and assume a renunciation that he would not have expected from Christians living in the midst of secular society. Even so, is it true to say that 'our old affections were mere selfishness'? The impression I gain from this and from other similar denigratory expressions is not that the writer really believes that our natural affections are totally corrupt but that he *feels* them to be a danger to a life of complete consecration. He voices a revulsion of the heart rather than a judgement of the head. It seems sometimes that he feels the body to be a dangerous enemy and to require the most rigorous discipline to prevent it from hindering the life of God in the soul. His penetrating theological vision is not balanced by an equal psychological understanding. He does not seem to recognize the truth in the words of his contemporary, Robert Browning, 'nor soul helps flesh more, now, than flesh helps soul'. Consider his teaching on detachment.

Our religious life is a death from earth. Death comes between you and all that is outside the house. You come here in order to die to the world more and more. Every day of your life must be a fresh mortification. You learn to be thankful for those things which mortify, to praise God for everything that helps you to be more detached. You come into the religious life in order to acquire this spirit of detachment, and what others have to learn by God's necessary providence you give yourself up to learn by an inspired vocation.[60]

He insists indeed that this detachment is only possible through the power and inspiration of the Holy Spirit, it is a by-product of love for God and his will. All the same there is a severity, an uncompromising quality, in his teaching that may chill the heart of some modern readers.

It is impossible for the modern reader to feel the impact of Fr. Benson's writings as his contemporaries did. He is haunted by the spectre of such thinkers as Marx and Freud with their criticisms of religion as illusion and particularly the other-worldly religion for which Fr. Benson stood. Had he been acquainted with the writings of either of these atheistic thinkers he would in all probability have dismissed them as voices of the world and therefore naturally hostile to the truth of God. But the contemporary Christian cannot so easily shut out these critical voices, and though he rejects the main thrust of their anti-religious views he is forced to acknowledge some truth in them and to modify his own thinking to accommodate it. Is there not a grain of truth in Marx's criticism of religion as leading to alienation? Does not the demand that men should suppress their natural instincts and passions sometimes lead them to feel hopelessly divided, the passive battleground of a war between flesh and spirit, between conscience and evil? Is there not some truth in Marx's assumption that religion by pointing to a heaven and hell where right and wrong will be rewarded has sometimes cut the nerve of the endeavour to make this world a juster one? Is there no truth whatever in Freud's idea of religion as a kind of neurosis, a compensatory illusion which makes the frustration by civilization of our sexual and aggressive instincts more bearable? The Christian in replying to these charges will be forced to make distinctions. Some religion is indeed unhealthy, neurotic and escapist, but this is not true of genuine religion. He will take great care if he uses such traditional terms as mortification and detachment to guard against their being misunderstood. He will take trouble to avoid exaggeration and to maintain a careful balance. And he is likely to find it difficult to be fair to this element in the teaching of Fr. Benson.

Part of the reason for our unease at Fr. Benson's stress on detachment from the world and antagonism to Satan is that the psychologists have made us more aware of the stages through which we pass in the development of real personhood. The psychotherapist in particular is concerned with people who have failed to achieve maturity because under the pressure of social expectation they have repressed important elements of themselves. His insistence on detachment and renunciation could strengthen repression and retard growth to maturity. To say this is to place Fr. Benson's writings in that large class of spiritual writings, which certainly includes those of St. John of the Cross, not suitable for indiscriminate reading. They are really intended for those who have attained a certain maturity and are committed to a life of prayer and to seeking God's will and his Kingdom.

The outstanding quality in Fr. Benson's spirituality is its rootedness in theology—theology understood as the knowledge of God, revealed in Jesus Christ through the Spirit. It is a loving knowledge that cannot rest content until at whatever cost all thought, all action, all life is brought into harmony with it; it is knowledge urging a person on to total commitment. Only the power of the Spirit welling up from within him can enable a man's whole life to be conformed to God; but man has to cooperate with the Holy Spirit, first by trust and then by acting against everything that hinders this commitment. Fr. Benson's theological vision is original and penetrating, but in his practical ascetic teaching he is content to follow tradition, interpreted somewhat strictly. But what he taught to others he practised himself. He fasted, he went without sleep, he endured cold, he refused to indulge his body. And if his general teaching today strikes us as extremely austere his dealing with individuals was tempered by compassion and gentleness towards human weakness and sin and by strong common sense. His letters to Fr. O'Neill with their frequent counsels about the care of his health in the Indian climate illustrate his practical prudence. He was well aware that most people could not with spiritual profit fast as he himself could. And there is evidence that in helping individuals in trouble and in hearing confessions he was loving and encouraging.

Some of those committed to the Christian journey see their life primarily in terms of warfare, of struggle for God and the Kingdom; others in terms of growth, growth in awareness of self, growth in the consciousness of God, growth in charity. The attitudes are not of course mutually exclusive, it is a question of one or the other predominating. The first type will find the idea of the following of Christ congenial, the image and the teaching of

Christ will tend to be the focus of their thought and their endeavour, they will try to bring their aims and actions into harmony with Christ. The second type will tend to see their Christian life as growing from within, as a work of grace to be fostered and responded to; they will be inward looking, scrutinizing their motives and acknowledging their unruly wills and affections as something that only God can order and rectify. A person of the first class will tend to face temptations by turning his attention away to thoughts and images which contradict them. For example a person tempted to anger might focus his attention upon the meekness and gentleness of Christ and in this way banish his angry feelings. One of the second type will use the gust of anger to strengthen his realization of what he is and his dependence on the grace of God; he will acknowledge his irascibility without giving way to it. To those of this type the saying of the staretz Silouan would be congenial, 'Keep your mind in hell and despair not'. Those of the first type would find spiritual nourishment in à Kempis's *Imitation of Christ*, those of the second would gain inspiration from the writings of de Caussade or Grou. The two classes overlap; no one would belong exclusively to either one or the other. Which of these ways is likely to attract a person depends partly on temperament, partly on the tradition in which he is brought up, but also partly on age and maturity. It is natural and appropriate for the young to see their Christian life in terms of struggle and warfare in the following of Christ. They have to decide what standards to follow, what ideals to make their own, and to refuse what is inconsistent with them; they have to struggle to discover their Christian identity. Later when they are firmly established in a Christian stance they will probably be drawn to look inwards, to face and come to terms with the bits of themselves that were either rejected or not allowed to develop, to realize the grace of God working within them and bringing about new life and growth.

Fr. Benson is too great a man to be fitted into either of these categories. Temperamentally he was a fighter and this disposition may have predisposed him to see the Christian life as a warfare with the prince of darkness. But this hostile attitude flowed quite as much from his theological vision of a world estranged from God and at enmity with him. Further the militant energy which permeates his writings is balanced by a strong contemplative and visionary spirit, a profound realization of the indwelling Godhead and of his total dependence on divine grace. He was wholly convinced of man's dependence on God and the powerlessness of human effort apart from the enabling Spirit. Unfortunately the force of his writings is weakened for the modern reader by his inveterate tendency to point the moral and urge to renewed effort. This is partly a consequence of the conviction which he shares with his fellow Tractarians that doctrine must find its appropriate expression in conduct and that theological renewal should issue in moral and spiritual transformation. It derives partly also, I think, from the evangelical piety of his upbringing with its tendency to moralize and improve the occasion. Had he been able simply to acknowledge the greatness and richness of God on the one hand and of human weakness and frailty on the other his writings would have been more persuasive, more uplifting, more truly liberating.

In an article quoted earlier Fr. Maturin spoke both of Fr. Benson's shyness and intense reserve and also of his need of and capacity for affection to which he allowed no human outlet. Had he been willing to receive the affection that many would have been glad to give, his humanity would have been enriched and he would have had more to give others. The truth of Fr. Maturin's insight is partly borne out by the fact that in his old age he did permit his warmth and affection on occasion to express themselves, especially towards the young. The American Fr. Spence Burton, who was to become Superior of the American Congregation of the Society and later Bishop of Nassau in the Bahamas, spent four years at Cowley when the Father was in his eighties. In an article written in 1930 he described the great love and affection which Fr. Benson showed towards him. On the day that he was made a novice he went to the Father, then a semi-invalid, to receive his blessing.

I found the Saint sitting in the cloister garth, bathed in bright sunshine from a cloudless blue sky. And there on the turf I knelt down beside him, and he blessed me. Then he leaned over, put his arms around me and kissed me.[61]

Other stories from this period which tell of bubbling gaiety and boyish exhilaration and a lively interest in secular affairs give further evidence of the rich and many-sided humanity which for many years he had kept under severe restraint. The account quoted in Canon Allchin's essay, given by one who in her childhood knew him well, shows a side of him which softens the grimness of the legendary portrait. The fact that he wrote a great deal of verse, even though of indifferent quality, sheds light on another side of him. The following lines translated by him from the French of Victor Hugo are here quoted because they give apt expression to a certain light-heartedness in his own spirit:

Let us learn like a bird for a moment to take
Sweet rest on a branch that is ready to break;
She feels the branch tremble, yet gaily she sings.
What is it to her? She has wings, she has wings.[62]

Had his self-restraint been less rigorous, had he been able to express more of his humanity in his personal relationships and in his writings and addresses, his vision and spiritual insight would have made a much more powerful impact on his contemporaries.

But probably to make this criticism is to be unrealistic and to desire in Fr. Benson qualities which being the man he was and living when he did could not be expected. Many holy people have in their later years deplored the austerities of their youth by which they ruined their health. Yes, but they followed the hard way along which they believed God was calling them; and had they evaded that call and chosen an easier road they would never have attained that sanctity which was their best gift to God and their fellows. It is likely that Fr. Benson in his youth was warned by wise and well-meaning friends to moderate his severity and perhaps be more sociable. But if such advice were indeed given and had it been heeded, he would have turned aside from the path which he believed passionately was his vocation; he would have been untrue to his vision and could not have become a great and inspiring religious teacher of the Church of England of his day— and perhaps of our own.

97

6

The Religious Life: Aspects of Father Benson's Teaching

R. Kemsley SLG

IT is as the Father Founder of the Society of St. John the Evangelist that Richard Meux Benson has been remembered. He gave to the revival of the religious life for men that stable basis by which it became viable and acceptable in the Church of England. The Society endured; Fr. Benson himself lived on and on; he became formidably venerable even within his own lifetime. But there is irony in the honour accorded him. It sits oddly on one who said:

The real danger and wretchedness of the religious community is when its dress has become a mark of honour in the world. Then indeed it is time to change it. It has outlived its day. . . . They [the religious orders] are of no use except the world is really hating and mocking them.[1]

When he returned from America and saw how the Society had become established in new buildings at Cowley he commented that 'my own life was more suited to the days of infancy, and I am glad to be out of the way of the world's welcome'.[2] He even went so far as to say that no institution should survive beyond the second generation for it would lose sight of its original purpose. He was not shirking the responsibility of a founder; authority came naturally to him with his sense of vocation, and he fully accepted the obligations and loneliness which its exercise entailed. Indeed even after relinquishing the office of Superior he remained an autocrat at heart, and undoubtedly this side of his nature invited the respect and reputation he acquired. But in the irony of the situation we have better access to Fr. Benson's complex character and may appreciate more clearly what he was trying to do.

He was, as he put it, 'a shocking Puritan', and not only with regard to religious art which was the context of the remark.[3] In worship he preferred 'that plainness which S. Bernard would have inculcated'.[4] He loved 'the bareness of the religious life', and advised Fr. O'Neill 'The poorer one's place of lodgement the better'.[5] He had a horror of anything that might thrust its apparent importance between himself and God, and he saw this danger particularly in any 'works' undertaken by religious. The religious life itself had to be put in its place:

We must remember that our life as Religious is not something over and above the ordinary Christian life. It is only the ordinary Christian life developed under such regulations as are rendered necessary for individuals, because the Church at large has fallen away from her true spiritual calling of conscious and habitual union with Christ.[6]

He had boundless and even contradictory hopes for the Society, but they were to be achieved incidentally, as it were, and by God. His uncompromising temperament and the fruit of his own prayer combined to shape his ideal, and while the Society was still in its infancy everything was still possible. He had no desire to imitate or reproduce traditional models of the religious life, although he had read and studied Holstenius' *Codex Regularum Monasticarum* and had first-hand knowledge at least of Jesuits whom he had known as a young man in Rome. The whole thrust of his vision was towards the future, but foreshortened because he felt himself to be living in the time of Antichrist, with the return of Christ, in some sense, a real possibility within his own life time. The resultant sense of urgency and immediacy was among the factors which led him to attempt to fuse together two apparently opposite vocations—that of a monastic community and that of a Society of Mission Priests. He would have been the first to admit that only God could enable the community to live such a vocation, and even then failure would be an inherent part of it. Estimated on his own strict terms we must allow that the Society has not succeeded, perhaps cannot succeed because of Fr. Benson's legacy to it—the tension between mission and monasticism, contemplation and action. And if he was himself disappointed we may surmise that he enjoyed the irony of finding more blessing there than in 'the world's welcome'.

For all his largeness of vision Fr. Benson was a Victorian clergyman who had interpreted his call to a deeper commitment to God as a call to the mission fields, who had experienced the contemporary social upheavals as the need for a new church in his parish at Cowley, and who gave to his community of 'quiet and industrious clergymen and laymen' an Englishness and appropriateness which cannot but bear witness to his own roots in that particular time and place. As Father Founder he inevitably recalls us to an achievement in Oxford towards the end of the nineteenth century. It is true, and remarkable, that within a decade of its inception the Society was sending men out to India and America, but for the significance of Fr. Benson to reach us a world and two world wars away we must perhaps, in fairness to him, cease to associate him exclusively with the Society which has preserved his memory. In temporarily forgetting 'the Father Founder' we may find that his teaching is capable of wider application and has a creative potential beyond that of founding an institution.

His own teaching about the religious life encourages us to do this because it is not about achieving anything—the conversion of the heathen, the foundation of a community, even the revival of something called 'the religious life'. It is about something much more fundamental—man's response to God, the *doing* of theology, in the sense of theology focused, prayed, practised and made visible in particular men and circumstances.

So we may begin with a conversation recalled by Fr. Congreve in which Fr. Benson, with characteristic truculence, challenged his suppositions and put the same subject in a different perspective.

One Sunday soon after I came, you invited me to walk with you to old Cowley, where you had promised to take the Evening Service, and to preach to the College boys. Here was my opportunity of gaining from you a clearer idea of the essential meaning of the religious life; so, as we walked, my enquiries began: 'I suppose, Father,' I said, 'that your object in founding the Society of St. John the Evangelist was to train the clergymen who join you for the work of missions at home and to the heathen abroad?' . . . 'No,' you replied; 'I do not think the object of our association in a Religious Community is to equip us to go out as missionaries. We do not come into our Community primarily in order to convert others, but rather with the desire, first of all, to be converted ourselves. Then, if by God's grace we are converted to Him, He may use us in missionary work, or in any other way that He pleases.'[7]

The religious is not called to do a special job or to be a particular kind of person: he is called by God *to* God. It follows that his call begins when he begins to discover who it is who calls him.

VOCATION AND REVELATION

The theme of the interaction of vocation and revelation is so integral to Fr. Benson's teaching on the religious life that it is not easily disentangled from other recurring themes. In the month-long retreats which he gave to the brethren at Cowley he explored, savoured and shared with them his hopes for the community. He turned their thoughts again and again to the contemplative vision of St. John the Evangelist—Christ dwelling in the bosom of the Father; his obedience making available all the energy and mystery of God's Trinitarian love; the personal call of Jesus to each one to enter into his 'sanctification through the truth'; the 'dreaminess' of the material world as against the substantial spiritual realities for which we long; ruthless detachment by which one's vision is clarified and all one's assumptions about the world turned inside out. 'If by God's grace we are converted to Him' (and surely it is the same conversion which St. Benedict made the foundation of the monastic life) then we are caught up in a movement determined by God and finding its impetus and end—which has no end—in him. Vocation is not merely an insight about myself but an identification and appropriation of the whole Christian revelation. It begins with the identification of God, so from the beginning it is a scandalous, even hopeless, business since God cannot be identified except as the one who is infinite and mysterious:

The nature of God is to man essentially incomprehensible, so much so that any statement or theory of God's Being which does not involve the element of incomprehensibility stands convicted of falsehood . . .[8]

In prayer man recognizes his creaturely limitations, but his need of the *transcendent* God comes to him as a call and promise:

. . . as I behold my vileness I learn to behold Thy glory. To behold Thee is to wonder, for Thou art beyond all power of sight, but in that wonder is our life, and gazing on Thee whom we see not, we grow into Thy likeness until we see Thee as Thou art.[9]

In a passage reminiscent of St. Augustine's *Confessions* Fr. Benson lays together the theologians' 'problem of revelation' and his own intimate and personal call:

God calls us to put away earthly things that we may behold Himself, and we cannot retain anything without shutting the door of heaven and shutting it for ever. O my God . . . Thou pleadest with me; Thou invitest me; Thou commandest me. O blessed be Thy Name that Thou dost invite; for my heart rejoices in the invitation of Thy love. But blessed be Thy Name that Thou dost command for indeed I had not dared even to love Thee unless I knew I must love Thee, or die. To love Thee had been too great a delight even to think of, unless I knew it as a necessity. O my God I cannot love Thee except in obedience to Thy bidding; for else I should not know Thee as my Creator and my God.[10]

He recognizes that it is God himself who has initiated the scandal of revelation, and knowledge of him is not some abstract information but knowledge within a relationship of love. It is therefore knowledge which grows with the relationship and which, because it is knowledge of God, increasingly recognizes that he *is* inaccessible and unknowable, and loves him the more for it. This leads us to an important feature of Fr. Benson's teaching which strikingly parallels Gregory of Nyssa's doctrine of *epektasis*. The inaccessibility of God is safeguarded by the soul's continually renewed realization that he is beyond her reach. A passage from St. Gregory's *Commentary on the Song of Songs* puts it succinctly:

The soul that looks up towards God, and conceives that good desire for His eternal beauty, constantly experiences an ever new yearning for that which lies ahead, and her desire is never given its full satisfaction. Hence she never ceases to stretch herself forth to those things that are before, ever passing from her present stage to enter more deeply into the interior, into the stage which lies ahead.
The soul having gone out at the word of her Beloved, looks for Him but does not find Him. She calls on Him, though He cannot be reached by any verbal symbol, and she is told by the watchmen that she is in love with the unattainable, and that the object of her longing cannot be apprehended . . . but the veil of her grief is removed when she learns that the satisfaction of her desire consists in constantly going on with her quest and never ceasing in her ascent, seeing that every fulfilment of her desire continually generates a further desire for the Transcendent.[11]

The result of such an approach for the 'doing of theology' in the religious life is chiefly that one is freed from idealizing it as a 'life of perfection' in any static sense. This traditional description can only apply to the continual movement of reaching out towards God in his perfection. Thus Fr. Benson:

. . . that the desires of our heart may be more and more magnified, and, as they are more and more magnified, so more and more may be fulfilled.

For our progress is not a progress which finds itself satisfied. Increasingly does it find its craving increase; but it is a craving which fills the soul with an intense consciousness of delight. For we know that it has its satisfaction. It is better to look forward to the satisfaction of God, than to have any satisfaction which could stop us on our way and hold us back from any of the divine perfections.

Let us learn, then, to cherish within ourselves a real longing for the divine glory. Do not look upon the religious life as a mere form of earthly existence, in which you may carry out a certain routine of religious exercises, and then be found fit for heaven because you were not fit for earth! . . . God calls, calls us to Himself, calls us onward and onward.[12]

Fr. Benson was familiar with the writings of St. Gregory, although this particular teaching is also profoundly and characteristically his own. It also reflects his deep love of scripture and intimacy with it, for it is not only a very theological approach but a very biblical one. It coincides with the biblical and monastic understanding of God's call and reminds us that the Bible had a central place in Fr. Benson's understanding of God's self-revelation. He was able to combine the Anglican and Protestant tradition (with its heritage of the King James Version) with the monastic and patristic tradition of *lectio divina*. We may recall the testimony of Viscount Halifax (himself drawn to the religious life, party to the original discussions about SSJE, and deeply formed by Fr. Benson) as one which might have come from Fr. Benson himself:

It was the Catechism, the Prayer Book, and, above all, reading portions of the Bible (especially the 6th, 13th, 14th, 15th, 16th and 17th chapters of St. John's Gospel, and St. John's Epistles) that formed my belief. This, coupled with the desire to believe what had always been believed by the Church and with the wish to be in harmony with and obedient to the teaching of the Catholic Church . . . not any love for or interest in ritual for its own sake, and the externals of the Church, was what shaped my life and determined its course . . . personal relation and union with our Lord, together with the keeping of His commandments, was the beginning and end of religion.[13]

The role of the Bible in forming Fr. Benson's teaching and in the life of the community can hardly be over-emphasized, but it rests on assumptions which we can no longer take for granted. Edwyn Hoskyns made this point in his introduction to *The Fourth Gospel*:

Westcott stood at the parting of the ways, for he belonged to a period in which the study of theology had not been altogether confounded with the study of history, and he lived before the time when the historians had driven the theologians almost completely out of the field. It was not possible, when Westcott was writing his commentary, for a leading English biblical scholar to comment on the Fourth Gospel, as for example Alfred Plummer was later to comment, or to regard it as offering primarily an opportunity for competent philological and historical exegesis, or for engaging in critical, conservative or radical historical speculation. When Westcott wrote his commentary the Fourth Gospel was still a great work of Christian Theology able to deliver up its secret only to those who were themselves sensitive to theological truth, prepared to assume that it is a 'good' book, and ready to listen to what it has to say without seeking to justify or defend it, or even to interpret or explain it, save on its own terms—in other words to those who were not on edge in its presence. To recover this temper we have to go back to Westcott, and perhaps we shall have to go back behind him to such a writer as the Rev. R. M. Benson.[14]

Fr. Benson was able to approach the Bible theologically because to him it did not tell of a closed episode of history so much as of an on-going process in which he was himself involved. This does not necessarily beg the questions which we must ask about the nature of the biblical documents and the material that is found in them. The Bible is the book of the people of God, and in reading it we may enter into their experience and the subsequent interpretative experience of the Church. God continues to be the One-who-calls. In the beginning he called creation into being, he called Abraham, he called Moses, he called David and the prophets. He called Adam and Noah and Ruth and Cyrus—particular people, his own people and the whole of mankind. In Christ the call became more explicit and insistent and carried with it the hope that man can and will respond and find his bliss and fulfilment in knowing and loving God. The story of God's people is not only traced in a succession of events—the series of attempts, misunderstandings, reappraisals, suffering and fidelity by which reality is touched, felt and, gradually, understood—it is also traceable in experience in which we are as yet too deeply involved to discern the 'event'. If this were not so God would not be the One-who-calls; we would not have to be roused and cajoled into leaping across the gap which separates us from him. In their daily recitation of the Psalms and meditation on scripture the young community found a language and a pattern with which to understand and interpret their own experience, which fed their imaginations and directed their desires.

The Bible can make no theological sense to us as long as we view it as a finished story, that is, a story without a future. The Bible only becomes comprehensible as a story when our present is related to history and the end of the story is seen to be a matter of our own future. Then when we, like the bride in the Song of Songs, realize the impossibility of our desire for God, our experience, relinquished, is seen more clearly and the deepening insight affords a clearer call. The on-going dialectic of vocation and revelation provides a dynamism by which the religious life is decisively orientated towards the future. For Fr. Benson this future is symbolized by the glorified Christ who gathers all creation into the life of God.

It is the duty of a Religious community to be really set apart for theology as a life, to live in the wisdom of the Incarnate Word.[15]

As one would expect, Fr. Benson sees the vocation to know God as being in the closest possible relationship to God's self-gift in Jesus Christ. But how are we to square the finality of Christ with a vocation whose momentum comes from the undisclosed future? The impossibility of man knowing God is not altered by the biblical and Christian insight that God is, at the least, personal. But it does mean that if by a paradox of grace God reveals himself, revelation is more than simply a disclosure, a window opened which might be closed again. Because God is personal he cannot reveal himself without giving himself, and he reveals and gives himself supremely in Christ. So the religious, far from aspiring to some 'higher' mystical path is dependent throughout upon his baptismal incorporation into Christ. The test of the validity of his vocation is not whether or not he 'succeeds' and attains to the beatific vision, but whether or not he is in accord with Christ and is a living member of the Church.

O then we must meditate upon the glory of the Lord as the glory revealing itself— not *having revealed* itself to the Apostles; but revealing itself first to the Apostles, and then by the living power of continuous inspiration to generation after generation, individual after individual through all the ages of the Church. And we must have this revelation of God just as truly given to us now as it did come on the Day of Pentecost to the Twelve.[16]

The very finality of Christ means that his revelation of God is qualitative as well as quantitative. It is as inexhaustible and irreducible as God himself. Similarly,

The vocation to the religious state is the voice of the Holy Spirit speaking once for all, but not as if there were no need to speak again, rather so as never again to cease to speak. The more carefully we keep our vows the more certainly shall we hear his voice.[17]

Just as vocation received as a gift and corollary of God's self-revelation draws a man into a living and on-going relationship with the Trinity, so the Trinitarian life involves him in a movement towards man. He becomes a giver and revelation of God to others. Fr. Benson draws attention to this pattern as he introduces the idea of mission work in the first chapter of the Rule, and in so doing he echoes Christ's words to the disciples in St. John's Gospel, 'as I . . . even so you', 'as Christ loved us, so must we also love one another'. Fr. Congreve was not altogether wrong in supposing that the object of the Society was 'to train the clergymen who join you for the work of missions at home and abroad', for the special responsibility of a religious community to make theology *visible*, to incarnate the love of God, was never far from Fr. Benson's mind. In 1859, before his decision to stay on at Cowley, he had written to the warden of St. Augustine's College, Canterbury, confiding in him his plans for a 'Collegiate Association' in Calcutta, which would 'be a witness for Christ to the heathenism around, and a place from which prayer should be continually ascending on behalf of the heathen'.[18] When the Mission House was opened in Marston Street he was at pains to explain to his parishioners what it was for, what happened during a 'retreat' and how they themselves might be involved in its life:

The hours of prayer will be regularly observed in the chapel of our Mission House, and I hope that many of the parishioners, although unable to attend, will lift up their hearts unto the Lord at such times wherever they may be. A few strokes of the bell will give notice what are the times at which they are said.

The chapel will not be open to ladies, but I shall be very glad if any of the men of the parish will at any time come in and worship along with us. The service is but a short one; and the midday prayer, occurring as it does just when the labouring men rest for dinner, they can easily, if they like it, arrange to come for that ten minutes to our chapel.[19]

However hidden and monastic the life, there was to be no mystique about it. The real test for a religious community is not its 'other worldliness' but its fruitfulness in love—which is why despite his own deeply contemplative nature Fr. Benson was mistrustful of the enclosed and contemplative life as such. Living waters—a favourite and powerful image of God's self-revelation —must either overflow or dry up altogether. It is again Fr. Congreve who gives us a revealing anecdote, this time not about the theory of the religious life, or of mission, nor even about the successful city missions in which the Fathers engaged, but about something small within the hidden life of the Society:

When I came as a Postulant to Cowley long ago (1873), I remember how the silence and real simplicity of the life impressed me; but a Postulant has 'long, long thoughts', grave questions to face, and doubts to settle with himself; and I think it was not the genuine austerity of the small family that settled my last doubt but the frank and cheerful kindness of one professed Father who sought me out in the strangeness of the first silent days, and took me for a walk in the country; he brought me back to my cell convinced. I had doubted whether a life all at a low temperature (so to speak), all in the shade . . . could be a truly Christian life; in Father O'Neill's friendship I found the unquestionable argument of light; where such a joyous generous charity shone, I recognized the indwelling of Christ, and there it was good for me to be.[20]

THE DYNAMICS OF DYING

A quotation from the *Rule*:

In our baptism we began to die unto the world, and received a grace enabling us so to do. This grace asserts itself most powerfully when the soul yielding to a divine call takes the vows of a Religious. Deadness to the world must henceforth be complete. Any conscious violation of such deadness becomes a grievous sin. Earthly hopes and fears are to be entirely put away. . . . The professed who gives himself wholly up to Christ should long, if it were possible, to be admitted to the crown of martyrdom. He must not look forward to such a possibility as an idle dream. He must gather strength for his daily life, to meet the difficulties of his ordinary duty, by the consideration of the martyr's fortitude. The deadness of the Religious is not dull apathy, but triumphant joy in the consciousness of possessing a true eternal life, from which nothing but the lingering life of the world holds us back.[21]

For Fr. Benson God's invitation, power and transcendance open up an infinite future for man which although not fully disclosed yet makes continuous demands upon him. 'The future' is Christ gathering all men and all creation in to God. This hope which is the essential witness of a religious community gives us a context in which to place his ruthless and categorical teaching about 'the deadness of the Religious'. It is also the necessary context for our misgivings as to whether such renunciation is either possible or truly Christian. 'One doubt pursues me still least all I *cannot* die';[22] Fr. Benson himself lamented that his contemporaries were less able than earlier generations to undertake traditional mortifications such as fasting. In the present generation we are not only aware that we are physically less tough than our predecessors. Psychology has made us aware of the power that the past has over us, that not only our personal experience but the whole racial history lives on in our unconscious. While witnessing to the freedom and power of God as against any form of psychological determinism we may yet ask whether 'eternal life' which is entirely discontinuous from natural life can have any content or value for us. It may be that self-denial simply follows naturally from a desire for God—the result of becoming increasingly absorbed in and consumed by the quest. As Fr. Benson put it, 'an Object has shined out before our souls; and when that Object has shined out it expels all other objects'.[23] But this is not sufficient defence against the charge of dualism and the suspicion that God and the world are incompatible—the nearer you get to one the further you are from the other. In fact Fr. Benson goes further and lays hold on the specifically Christian mystery of life out of death. The future is so different that only death is radical enough to free us for it, yet we are not strangers to this future because our physical world and our communion with each other are included in it. In the incarnation, death and resurrection of Jesus and in the outpouring of the Holy Spirit we are shown that this 'future' is the life of God himself; in baptism we begin ourselves to become conformed to it.

From the first the Church regarded martyrdom as the highest and clearest witness that a Christian could give to his faith in Christ. By martyrdom he made baptism into Christ's death a physical reality; he became like Christ in that he could say deliberately and directly in the very face of death, 'O death, where is thy victory? O death, where is thy sting? . . . Thanks be to God which giveth us the victory through our Lord Jesus Christ' (1 Cor. 15). The Eucharist celebrated on the tombs of the martyrs was a powerful sign of their, and the Church's, incorporation into

Christ through his death. As persecution abated and literal martyrdom became less of a possibility its power as an epitome and symbol of triumphant identification with Christ did not diminish. Something of the significance of martyrdom was predicated of the monastic life, described as a 'white' or bloodless martyrdom, no less uncompromising and demanding for being less dramatic and more sustained than 'red' martyrdom. Fr. Benson's emphasis on 'life-long mortification' must be seen in this tradition and, like martyrdom, directly related to baptism and the Christian's incorporation into Christ. Inevitably martyrdom focused the attention on Christ's death, imitated and appropriated in a way which could be equivalent to baptism. But the fellowship with Christ and the power which springs from 'sharing' his death is of a new order, involving the transformation of the whole man and participation in all his mysteries. For Fr. Benson this means that the death of Christ is never seen in isolation from his resurrection and glorification and that the 'deadness of the Religious life' cannot be isolated from the outpouring of the Holy Spirit on the whole Church.

Fr. Benson very often compared the religious life to entry into the tomb. When the door of the Mission House chapel closed on the community assembled for a profession ceremony the brother or father to be professed was to think of the stone being rolled across the door of the sepulchre. Henceforward all his expectation and aspiration for life and fulfilment were to be fixed on Christ and the new life which sprang from the tomb. The Rule made the monk's cell another focus for this hope:

The cell is the grave in which the Religious is buried to the world, and the paradise in which he finds heaven begin. On entering the cell look to the form of the Crucified, realize your union with Him, and say: 'Here will I dwell, for I have a delight therein.'[24]

To understand the force of this symbolism and the cause for such delight we must turn to Fr. Benson's treatment of the resurrection stories, referring particularly to *The Final Passover*, vol *IV*.

Firstly, the resurrection stories say something vital about God's relationship to the physical and material world. To Fr. Benson there was no question of mere resurrection 'appearances' or of explaining the stories solely in terms of the dawning experience of the Church. They were not simply stories which the disciples told to each other to encapsulate and convey their insight into the meaning of Christ and his death. Neither did they tell of visionary experience—at the very least the words meant what they said and referred to objective events known through the ordinary physical senses. The resurrection of the body of Christ was as essential to Fr. Benson as the Word becoming flesh, for it speaks of flesh becoming spirit. Seen in the context of the incarnation the resurrection stories may not be relegated to the realm of miracle and abnormal occurrences. Rather they are the vindication of the true order of things in which only God is absolute and acts with freedom within space and time, upon the very stuff of our limitation and relativity. We are so used to turning space and time into absolutes that we dismiss the resurrection as unnatural rather than alter our frame of reference. We forget that all our criteria are relative to each other and convey meaning only within their own terms. But 'God does not exist in space. Space is merely the medium through which His operation is spread out before us for the apprehension of our senses. Rather is it God in whom space exists, the creature of His will.'[25] Just as a physical body is required by our concept of personhood so the Lord's resurrection body is simply the proper expression of himself, 'As the flint stone, clarified into glass, no longer impedes the faculty of sight, but helps it, so the material particles raised in glory no longer confine, but seem to transmit and communicate the forces of the glorified Body to which they belong. . . . Now in His resurrection He is His own true self, both in Body and Soul.'[26] Thus for the religious 'leaving the world' involves leaving the world's habitual way of viewing material things, leaving behind the assumption that material things are somehow more real than spiritual things, and affirming that both flesh and spirit must be taken entirely seriously if the one is to become the apt expression of the other.

Secondly, the resurrection was not a private event. Fr. Benson draws attention to the fact that although the grave clothes could not bind Christ (they were left undisturbed) and the stone at the door of the sepulchre could not imprison him nevertheless there was a great earthquake and an angel rolling back the stone. These events summoned witnesses to the mystery so that from the beginning the resurrection stories were also the Church's stories. The freeing of Christ from death constituted the birth of the

Church, and the stories tell about people becoming the Church. They bring us as close as we can come to the original experience and challenge us to be similarly changed. To enter into the sepulchre with Christ is to let ourselves become the Church, 'taking your place in the mighty multitude' and becoming in turn changers of reality—as the disciples who told of the resurrection changed the course of history. Death with Christ involves death to what is merely private, the beginning of community and growth.

Thirdly, just as Fr. Benson saw perfection not as a state but as a progressive movement into God, so the resurrection is not Christ's final achievement but the initiation of a new mode of life. At its most striking and graphic this means that Christ can be said to *grow*. Here the story of Christ eating with the disciples after the resurrection has vital significance, for the fish and the honeycomb which he eats vanish with him, having become part of his body 'in order to show the reality of that abiding identification with Himself into which it was thus mysteriously taken'.[27] Christ's risen body can 'communicate its own spiritual character to that which is earthly',[28] taking material things and raising them to its own glory. This is what happens in baptism and this is what the religious lays hold upon in his profession. It is true that he lives in the tension between the 'already' of Christ's resurrection and the 'not yet' of creation's identification with him—but it is the same tension which creates the Church. The Church, when truly herself, is the body of Christ in a more than metaphorical sense. The members of the Church are transparent to his will just as his risen body is. They are caught in the same paradox of flesh and spirit, they manifest the same weakness as glory, and have substance in time and space in the 'short time' of the last days. The particular role of religious is to anticipate here and now the drawing of all creation into 'mysterious identity' with Christ and experience in themselves with particular acuteness the contradiction and pain that it is *not yet* so. 'Look to the form *of the Crucified*, realize your union with Him and say, "Here will I dwell, for I have a delight therein".'

Lastly, like St. John, Fr. Benson places the resurrection and the giving of the Holy Spirit in very close relationship to each other. Thus it is not only that Christ in his risen body draws creation to himself, but that he communicates to us the impulse and transforming power of the Holy Spirit. This is the principle behind the sacraments, especially baptism and the Eucharist, leading to sanctification and placing us in the same relationship to the Father as Christ. It is there, in the intimate life of the Trinity, that the 'imitation of Christ' begins—growing compassion leading to self-sacrifice in which one is sustained again and again by the Holy Spirit. Thus entry into the tomb with Christ and 'death' in the religious life is not something which occurs just once; it is a repeated rhythm into which more and more of one's life is assimilated and by which, through the Holy Spirit, one becomes conformed to the life of Christ. The pattern and clue to the life of the Trinity lies in Christ's death. The giving of the Holy Spirit through his resurrection makes the link, ties the knot as it were, between man at his most helpless in death and deprivation and the life of God at its very source. Death—crucifixion—is suddenly given a future and becomes, in the self-giving love of God, a source of holiness and blessing. It is surely this which explains why Fr. Benson loved to dwell on the glorified wounds of Christ, still visible in his risen body—'not an element of weakness was there in the Passion which does not live on as a form of joyous brilliancy in the risen body of Jesus'.[29] All the dying that we can do, all the mortification and entering into the tomb, as well as all the embittering and unchosen anguish in the world, is already there in the heart of God. All we can do in worship and thanksgiving is 'give Him only fragments as it were of His own Passion'.[30] But, as in the life of the Holy Trinity itself, we must at least do this for in us, as in God, the Holy Spirit gives the energy and the will to love to the point of death.

Our retreat into the grave of Jesus must be a surrender of ourselves with the fullness of faith in the life of Jesus. To the natural eye the Religious Life is the sphere of death; to the spiritual man it is the manifestation of Divine Life in fuller power. As the Holy One saw no corruption, for the Divine Life was with the Sacred Body, so the Divine Life is with us: if we retire into His grave, we retire into the life of God. It is this life of God that fills the soul, that thus dies, with holy joy. It is the life of the Holy Ghost . . . It was 'by the Eternal Spirit that Jesus offered Himself to God,' and we must offer ourselves through the same Spirit. We must do it; and yet it is the Holy Ghost who must inspire the impulse and sanctify the act. He who calls us thus to Himself will enable us to answer the call.

We must realise that our vows are the living bond by which the Holy Ghost would knit us to Christ the Life.[31]

CONFLICT AND COMMUNITY

Man was formed in the image of the Blessed Trinity, with a social nature representative of the Being of his Creator. When man was put into the world it was said, 'It is not good for man to be alone'.[32]

So Fr. Benson began an instruction on life in community and went on to explain how human society has so far fallen short in reflecting the divine image that social life has actually become man's greatest source of suffering, difficulty and danger. However, the life which Christ opens up for man in God is again a *social* life and finds its expression in the redeemed and regenerate society of the Church. The aim of a religious community is to 'realize that which God intended for the Church'[33]—to be the place where the Trinitarian law of self-giving love can operate most freely and fully. It is to be a shelter from the world conditioned as it is by the fall, defined and fenced off by the vows of poverty, chastity and obedience to make room for the sanctifying power of the Spirit. It enables its members to enter into that communion and fellowship with each other which is among the deepest and most godlike of human needs. But at the same time its very existence involves them in conflict at a number of levels.

In the first place there is conflict with the world. Fr. Benson uses 'the world' in the Johannine sense of the fallen world, the world which was made by God but does not know him, which has turned in on itself and rejected all but a dislocated and barren relationship to him. The world in this sense is the object of the first renunciation in the rite of baptism. The vows of a religious reaffirm this renunciation and imply sharp criticism of the world's values. And the world by its very nature cannot understand the theological basis of the vows.

In missionary work particularly there were innumerable decisions to be made at odds with the world's values. By eschewing quick results and allowing a life of dedicated poverty and Christian priesthood to make its own slow impact the religious could give direct witness to his faith in God. This undramatic conflict does not depend on censoriousness or indifference but upon that delicate mixture of humour and principle by which faith is maintained *in* the world, but in a dimension of which it cannot but be ignorant. When Fr. Benson writes from on board ship, for instance, we find it uninterrupted and unimpaired even when the world is at very close quarters. During the voyage to America in 1880 he had been saying the office 'with porthole open, and my face turned towards the great expanse of waters':

It is enough to make a saloon or any other place happy, only one does wish that one could make people round about know something of the happiness that they might have in the Psalter if they would. How strange it is to think that one can have such an intense secret of happiness, and that the people round about should be so utterly ignorant of the pleasure within their reach.[34]

Ten years later on the voyage to Bombay we find him at once keenly interested and involved in all that is going on, and yet treasuring his solitude:

There are a very considerable number of nice people on board. One table is entirely occupied by missionaries. My own table is chiefly military. Our Bible-class of which I spoke has incorporated some additional members. There have been constant athletics and concerts, but they have not disturbed my routine of life, not has the betting on the day's run. I believe the obstacle race was a very good one yesterday. . . . The people on board generally get to bed in very fair time, and I have enjoyed the deck very much when I have had it to myself.[35]

Or it might simply be a matter of retaining a sense of humour:

My dear O'Neill, I'll write to you in verse!
All round me is a scene of dripping woe
Wasting this gay saloon. My thoughts unroused
Will freeze, like mental chilblains, if in prose.
Upon the stilts of metre let me rise
Above the mire of natural circumstance . . .[36]

Fr. Benson may have dreamt of establishing a novitiate in China, forcibly cut off from distractions and 'far away from the many molestations of England',[37] but he knew very well that the real battleground and the longest conflict with the world takes place within the monastery itself. For all the powerful symbolism of death and 'leaving the world' at profession, the religious is in practice still to a large extent 'world' himself. He only sees that this is so as the application of poverty, chastity and obedience, the demands of the common Rule, unmask his selfishness and his own small world turned in on itself. Here Fr. Benson's teaching about progress, continuous conversion in response to the continuous call of God, takes on a different aspect for it reveals God's mercy. It is not only that God is infinite, and so we can never 'arrive' but that he tempers the insight he gives and the demands he makes to what we are able to receive. 'We cannot bound into the depths of God at one spring; if we could we should be shattered, not filled. God draws us on.'[38] Community life is the scene and instrument of this gradual process. It is a constant opportunity to set aside individual desires and ambitions in favour of the common good, thus each small world of intro-version and isolation is gradually broken into and broken up, and real co-operation and community begin to emerge. Fr. Benson expected community life to be testing and difficult, as well as exhilarating, because nobody has 'arrived', everybody is growing. Certainly it is a sign of what will be, and it has a strength which unites its members scattered over four continents—already there are glimpses of what love can mean in terms of mutual under-standing, respect and the gift of freedom to each other. But struggle and conflict do not contradict this, they show that the sign is real and effective.

Fr. Benson expected a religious community to be poor and disparaged ('if the Society in any place is poor, look to God to do great things by it'[39]); he feared nothing so much as success and subtle reassimilation to the world as a result. He did not share the romantic's idyllic view of the monastic past but learnt from it how easy it is for religious communities to slip into religious world-liness and be tragically deflected from their prophetic vocation. He shared something of his fellow churchmen's Protestant sus-picions in this respect. He was not one to accept the *status quo* and one wonders how he would have fared in a Church where the tradi-tion of the religious life was well-established and unbroken. As it was, misunderstanding and opposition were precisely the circum-stances to encourage him. Even so discreet a 'monastic habit' as a black cassock attracted jeering attention in Oxford in the 1870's; the world could not have paid him a higher compliment.

A religious community by its very existence also finds itself in conflict with the Church. If the Church had 'realized that which God intended' for her there would be no need for religious com-munities; the Church herself would be the community of self-giving love, imaging the social life of the Trinity, and 'manifest-ing Christ in a fallen world'. But the Church has failed.

It mingled itself with the world in a way very different from that which was the divine Will. It has been the divine intention that this society, keeping itself separate from all contact with the world, should absorb the world into itself. But on the contrary this society chose rather to yield itself up to various forms of contact and alliance with the world, and so it became absorbed in the world.[40]

The religious community's conflict with the world has therefore to include conflict with the Church. Is it then a church within the Church? a *corps d'élite*, pure and uncontaminated? If that were so then its life would be cut off at the source, it would be a sect, perhaps morally 'better' than the Church but 'uncontaminated' by the life of the body of Christ. Fr. Benson's teaching will never allow of this interpretation.

Let us change the image from that of the Church as a pyramid with religious at the top, to that of a sphere with religious at the heart. They are separated from 'the anxieties which fret the outer surface of the Church's life' in order to 'abide in union with Christ, realizing the stability of the Kingdom of Christ amid all the varieties of outer change'.[41] Their place at the heart of the Church is a hidden one with all the gospel qualities of the salt and the leaven in a lump of dough. When the 'edges' of the Church are frayed in an age of unbelief this heart and focus is doubly important. The religious community will feel if anything more deeply the sin and suffering of the Church because, as in the conflict with the world, it is part of it. Its members' protest does not lead them to opt out but to engage very simply and radically in the Church's own vocation. Like the Church they must see their existence as essentially a temporary measure and hope to find their fulfilment in becoming ultimately unnecessary. The Church will herself realize God's intention for her and the whole of human society will be caught up in the order and energy of the life of God. It is the vision of St. John in the Book of Revelation: 'And I saw no temple therein: for the Lord God Almighty, and the Lamb, are the temple thereof'.

Finally, Fr. Benson insists that a religious community must face supernatural conflict with Satan as the work for which it is peculiarly fitted and which stamps the vocation as truly coming from God. Direct, clear-sighted and intensely costly knowledge of evil does not come from the 'Father of Lies' but from God before whom alone the full extent of evil is laid bare and borne. It is a mystery, seen in Gethsemane, in the temptation story, in the dereliction on the cross and in the descent into hell, which Christ shares with his Church. This conflict is then more than a struggle for personal salvation or sanctity, it is part of the non-private character of vocation and springs from the community's place in Christ and at the heart of the Church. This is so most starkly in a contemplative community—and Fr. Benson's appreciation of the seriousness of the conflict contributed to his feeling that such a vocation was 'scarcely conceivable' in his own time. At the same time he saw clearly that 'it is the contemplative life gazing up to God and doing battle with Satan, which is the essential character-istic of all Christian life'.[42]

Just as the Christian stands before God 'in Christ' entering into Christ's relationship to the Father, so he joins battle with Satan as a victor by virtue of Christ's victory. Ascetic conflict with the world is a training which may enable him to discern the true nature of the conflict with evil and help him to endure in it, but the issue ultimately depends on God. 'Gazing up to God' and 'doing battle with Satan' are not two activities, so that he must do first one and then the other, but a single act finding its focus, again, in the glorified wounds of Christ. Once more we are reminded of the parallelism in St. John's gospel: ' . . . as I . . . even so you. . .'; and the paradox which accompanies it, 'already' but 'not yet'. 'Gazing up to God' the Christian sees the accomp-lished work of Christ, the wounds suffered, the Spirit given, the revelation made. His seeing is not abstract or alone but in the covenant and company of the Church. He becomes himself one who suffers, one who gives the Spirit, one who reveals God, and he experiences in this becoming the agony of 'not yet' and the force of Satan's opposition. He is purified and strengthened in a way which is entirely God's. Such experience and conflict can only occur in community, whether it be the religious com-munity, the Communion of Saints, the visible Church or, sheerly and secretly, community in the being of God. Further it is a conflict which must ultimately issue in that community which will embrace all mankind.

CONCLUSION

Things are very different with us now from what they were some few hundred years back. Then the intellect was calm, inactive, residing in muscular bodies which needed restraint and attenuation in order to refinement. Now the nervous system is so much fretted by the excite-ment of life, our own and our parents' lives. We have neither the same logical subtlety, nor the same simple childlike gaze, in which former generations might live. Our bodies will not bear the same external discipline which they could. Then too we have a duty towards the world around us. . . . We must take a thing as a whole, and not imagine that we can reproduce a part of it.[43]

So Fr. Benson writing probably in 1896 to a religious who had enquired about the contemplative life. The realism which has to reckon with stress and complexity seems to belong more to the twentieth than the nineteenth century. He even seems to antici-pate some of our reactions to *his* teaching about the religious life. He was in fact wrongly pessimistic about the revival of the con-templative religious life, for only ten years later just such a Sisterhood was founded under the guidance of SSJE. But he was surely right that 'we must take a thing as a whole, and not imagine that we can reproduce part of it'. One of the problems of his teaching is that he does not give a separate rationale of the religious life, and none of the aspects which we have considered here can be applied exclusively or definitively to religious. He takes the Christian life whole, and it is only as this whole is applied fearlessly to that part which is known as 'religious' that it acquires a distinctive identity. To take his own teaching whole is not to imagine that we can imitate any particular part of it but to catch something of his vision and find in this new perspective that we are perhaps not so far from the Father Founder.

7

'When All are Christians None are': Church and Mission in the Teaching of Father Benson

R. M. C. Jeffery

ONE of the major sources of information into the missionary thinking of Fr. Benson lies in the large number of letters which he wrote to Fr. O'Neill and the others who pioneered the work of the Society of St. John the Evangelist in India. It was quite remarkable that so soon after the foundation of the Society the work in India was begun. The quotation which heads this essay comes from one of these letters. It is a passage which brings together many strands of his thought about mission.

Whether India will ever be a Christian country may be very doubtful. I cannot say I wish to see it. The experience of Christianizing countries leads one to believe that the country is Christianized at the expense of souls, and when all are Christians none are. We must look for Christianity to grow up in India in some very different form from that of the West. Let us hope that it will be a form of never-ceasing stand-up fight with the world around.[1]

Here many aspects of Fr. Benson's ideas of mission come together. His great disapproval of Christendom, which made the Church dependent on the State, leads him to suspect 'successful Christianity'. To be a Christian is not to accept the standards of the world around, yet at the same time the faith must be expressed through the culture in which it is placed. The tension here is one which he would see implicit in the doctrine of the Incarnation. The role of mission is not to do God's work for him but to obey Christ and through a life of prayer to be a channel of his Holy Spirit, who alone brings life. Fr. Benson's theology of mission springs from his study of scripture and the early Church together with his reflections on the missionary expansion of the nineteenth century.

The Society of St. John the Evangelist is a Society of Mission Priests and Brothers and it is this word 'mission' which permeates much of Fr. Benson's thinking. In formulating his ideals for the Society devoted to prayer, study and mission work, he saw an urgent need for the conducting of parish missions, the establishment of mission centres (especially in London) and for foreign mission. He had himself expected to go as a missionary to India but had remained in Cowley in obedience to his bishop. The life of the mission priest wherever he was would always express that following of Christ which involved obedience and suffering.

CHRISTENDOM

In order to understand Fr. Benson's concept of mission we need to come to terms with his deep dislike of Christendom and the missionary methods which sprang from it. The essential nature of the Church was to follow Christ and be like him. As he was depised and rejected so the Church would be. Compromise with the standards of the world would lead to a debasement of the Christian Faith. The Church has succumbed to this desire for worldly standards far too much. 'When Constantine took up the Cross, the Church laid it down.'[2] The desire for power and authority has meant that the Church has denied the very gospel it was supposed to be proclaiming. The miracle is that Christ still sees fit to operate through the Church:

It is difficult to look through the past centuries of Christendom, and realise how utterly at variance is the world-empire of the Church with the intention of Christ. If we do so, our wonder then remains how Christ can have been willing all along to recognize as His Vine such a system resting upon earthly greatness as stifled the heavenly respiration of the Church from the days of Constantine onwards.[3]

He saw that this was the trouble with much of the missionary expansion of the nineteenth century:

The worldly power of Christian nations which has been used for the maintenance of missions has been, perhaps, one of the greatest hindrances to the advance of the Church throughout the world. National pride can more easily send a gunboat to obtain toleration, than individual charity can supply the means for carrying on such mission works with efficiency; but if political influence may sometimes open a country to the voice of a missionary, the same power will probably hinder much of the supernatural support which would have been given from Heaven to a missionary toiling in the simple discipleship of faith.[4]

Christendom has been a great evil and diverted and twisted the way of true Christian mission and discipleship. There was a need to find a new and better way.

MISSION

For Fr. Benson the task of the Church and of Christians is above all to give glory to God. One main way in which this is done is by mission. For him, as for many after him, the inspiration for this comes from the Johannine text 'as the Father hath sent me, even so send I you' (John 20.21). This is much more a matter of obedience and giving glory to God than of gathering large numbers into the Church. The purpose of mission is that the Holy Spirit may make God known. To make masses of converts might well mean succumbing to Christendom. So he writes:

Not that we are to expect that there will be a great conversion of the nations. I think that is just the old European idea which we have to get rid of. Missions were measured more by converts who came than by the truth of the Holy Ghost Who went forth, but Who was sadly crippled in His going forth by the earthliness of the organisation of the Western Church. We may hope for a little nucleus of Christian life to be eliminated from the effete mass of Eastern and Western Christendom, and then for such a flash of light as shall speak home to hearts whom God hath called. It must be a little flock who shall win the kingdom at the last.[5]

What then of the dominical command to preach the gospel to all nations? Is this to be neglected? Far from it. Fr. Benson argues in his strange paper *The Virgin Birth of Our Lord, the Foundation of the Christian Religion* that the very existence of many nations is part of the Fall and that the new humanity offered in Christ must include all nations.

Had it not been for the wound of original sin whereby the unifying life of God was lost, mankind would have remained in absolute unity. We may conceive that the developments of nations and individuals would have multiplied and specialized the common consciousness of joyous power, for whatever was the gain of any one would have been the possession and the delight of all. All the antagonisms of interest, nationality, and every other distinction would have been avoided. Mankind would have spoken one language, being indwelt by the Word of God. Mankind would have been bound together in one Spirit of Love.[6]

This mission is in order that the true humanity of mankind might be restored. This idea has implications both for mission and unity, for Fr. Benson is clearly seeking the unity of mankind as the aim of mission and the unity of the Church as foreshadowing it. It is a unity which can only be achieved by the blood of Jesus.

The unity was broken up into individualities, and none can be restored until the Bride of Christ formed by the Blood of the Second Adam shed from His Holy Side has gathered the faithful in the full power of His own Resurrection. We cannot regain His glory by outward oneness but we must look to regain outward oneness by the inward indissoluble vitality of His glory which we are called to share. His Blood as the formative principle of the New Humanity lifted us up by grace into that unity of supernatural life.[7]

Civilization has developed by the breaking up of humanity through the corrupt blood of Adam. Only the blood of the Lamb can bring mankind together again. Jesus through his Incarnation took upon himself the common humanity of all the nations. Unlike the rest of mankind there was nothing in him to limit 'His character, or His affections or His interests.'[8] By his Virgin Birth Jesus is the 'seed of the collective humanity' which because of his divine origin is not corrupted by the sin of man. So there is nothing in any race of man which he does not share as 'Son of Man'. Because each nation has been created by the loss of some essential element of the perfect nature of man so also every nation contains some element which all need if Christ is to be seen in his fullness. Thus the full power of Christ's humanity cannot be seen until every element in man's nature, which is at present distributed throughout the nations, is brought together in the Church.

The most savage and degraded nations have some element of human nature which makes them what they are. They are not only capable of being restored in Christ but their restoration is essential to the integrity of Christ's glorified Humanity, because the virginal humanity which He has assumed comprises all those elements which have been derived from the original humanity of Adam, our common father.[9]

Here then is the motive for mission. Home mission is not enough because the Church must be formed out of all nations and it cannot be complete until every nation and race has made its own contribution.

We must look for the dark races of Africa to shine with the glory of the Divine countenance. India must wake up from her dreams to worship the Personality of the Incarnate God. China must go forward to the hope of heaven. . . . The dwarfs of Equatorial forests and the cannibals in islands of the sea have their individualizing inheritance. . . . and the Blood of Christ cannot assert the fullness of its redemptive power until it has made manifest in them that speciality of renewing grace whereby they may claim their part in the inheritance of the Saints, as members of Himself, the Second Adam.[10]

The Apostles must therefore go to all nations. But for Fr. Benson the key passage is indeed Chapter 20 of St. John's Gospel. There Jesus imparts the divine life to the Apostles. By being sent out in the Spirit they would not be separated from the divine life; for at the heart of mission lies the procession of the Holy Spirit through the world. They do not have a separate mission from Christ; they share in his mission. It should perhaps be noted here that this is the great theme of much current writing on the theology of mission.[11]

He sends them forth into the world by taking them up into the very participation of that original commission which He has received. That commission lives on in them, as the life which is in the head regulates the actions of the hand not by mechanical impact but by vital energy.[12]

When Jesus breathes on the disciples, he gives them his new life. As God breathed into the nostrils of the old Adam, so the Spirit brings his new life to his people. This gift of God is corporate rather than individual. The Church is a corporate entity in Christ validated by his presence and his Spirit.

It is just because Fr. Benson holds such a high doctrine of the Church with its strong sense of mission and its representative character that he is very concerned about the quality of the Church. Quality is immeasurably more important than quantity. Those who are truly united to Christ will be Christlike people. As Jesus was rejected so the Church will be rejected. As Jesus must die, so Christians must be dead to the world. What happens to Jesus happens to his Church. The Church will grow but not necessarily in numbers:

The growth of the Church is not a mere extension of Christian doctrines or principles but of Divine Life. This Divine Life does not conquer and inspire the world by remoulding the world, so that the world may take possession of it, but it takes possession of the world, and by so doing remoulds it.[13]

He would have found the whole 'Church growth' school of modern missiology very distasteful.

> Church statistics as to numerical growth at any particular time are altogether worthless. We do not count so many Christians against so many Buddhists; we cannot count how many Christians are by this time stablished in the security of Jerusalem; nor can we tell how many, or rather how few, of those who are called Christians upon earth are really to be considered as having part in the city. . . .[14]

The vision he has then is of Christ in his mystical body the Church rebuilding a new humanity, living in the Spirit of God and representing all nations. But the Church will not thereby necessarily be large and popular— rather the reverse:

> The rejection did not cease with that judicial act upon the Jewish nation. The offer of God would be gradually made to all the nations of the world. This gradual offer would fill up the lengthened period which must elapse before the manifestation of His Advent in glory. As He was rejected of the Jews so His Church would be continually rejected by the world. In every nation and in every generation there would be some who would accept.[15]

So the mission must continue.

THE CHURCH

The Church is therefore to be the channel of divine life mediated through the apostolic ministry and the sacraments. It is a corporate body in which we all share and in which we all need each other. As all nations must be in the Church so all sorts of people and gifts are needed within it. No number of individual saints can be as effective as the corporate life of the Church in which the different gifts of each person are used by Christ.

> In the Body of Christ, we have each our special function, and that function is itself diversified according to the purpose of our creation; and whatever be our individual vocation our work must be the outcome of the mind and will of Christ acting through us. He is both the Head and the Heart of the Body, being both God and Man. We can then none of us do the work which Christ assigns to any one else.[16]

Fr. Benson uses many biblical images, some of them rather unexpected, in his thinking about the Church. We see that usually what he says about Jesus he also applies to the Church. One of his most insistent themes is the Johannine one of the separation of the Church from the world. This separation does not imply that the Church remains detached and uninvolved in the ordinary concerns of society. We know very well with what immense energy he promoted not only wide-ranging educational and welfare work but also cultural activities aimed at enriching the lives of ordinary men and women in his parish such as horti-cultural societies, entertainments and concerts. What this separation really means is perhaps best conveyed through the picture of 'the Doors being shut'. It is an image he uses more than once but which he examines fully in *Life Beyond the Grave*. There he has a paragraph entitled 'The Cloistered Church' where he states: 'The Church of God must be shut off from the influence of the world if she is to appreciate the powers of the hidden life.'[17] It is to this cloistered Church that Jesus shows his risen glory. If the Church is to live in God it must be open to him. This is a way of speaking about what Bonhoeffer calls the concern with the ultimate and the realization that all other than God can only at best be the penultimate. The Johannine view of the world is right when compared with the ultimacy of God. The doors must be shut. Christians must have the right priorities.

Elsewhere Fr. Benson spells this out in other ways. The temptation of the Church as seen in much missionary work is to so adapt the gospel to the culture of the age that it ceases to be the gospel. The scandal of the cross is avoided:

Man will not accept Christ unless he can adapt Christ so as to suit the fancies and desires of each successive age. In order to be forgiven man must become conformed to Christ; but he tries to conform Christ to himself. There is a living power in Christ which makes men afraid. Man, therefore, seeks to reduce Christ to his own position of deadness that he may accept Christ without inconvenience or apprehension.

. . . Therefore the world is continually inventing new forms of Christianity. Every such endeavour is for the purpose of eliminating the strictness of the Divine requirements from the religion of Christ. In all these ways they nail Jesus to the Cross! The devotional life of Jesus, His love to the Father, suits them not. The spiritual earnestness of Jesus, the discipline of the earthly nature, perfecting it for the Kingdom of Heaven, suits them not. They would like a heaven on earth, but they have no desire to quit earth for heaven above. . . . Anyhow they will try and adapt Jesus to the needs of their own age, by nailing the Eternal to the Cross![18]

In thinking about motives for mission the risk of reducing the gospel simply to the philosophy of the age is always present. The scandal of the gospel must remain. It is here that we see what he means by 'the world'. It is everything in life which expects conformity to itself rather than conformity to Christ. When the Church seeks conformity to anything other than Christ it clearly denies its own inner nature.

MISSIONARY METHODS

What then are the methods by which the Church proclaims Christ and makes his kingdom known? It was not so much methods as a way of life which he sought to establish:

I do not think we have any new form of mission work to invent; but we have to train ourselves patiently for this mission life, and to live patiently and prayerfully, so that another generation may enter into the fruits of our labours.[19]

There were three expressions of mission, of which, although he did not condemn them totally, he was clearly very suspicious. They were public preaching in the streets, Church buildings and schools. It may be as well to look at these negatives before examining the positive side of his missionary thinking.

Preaching in the streets did not achieve much:

I believe Indian missionaries are getting generally to feel that bazaar preaching is of next to no good. Our Lord and the Apostles never carried on a system of what we should nowadays call outdoor preaching. Of course in accordance with the habits of the country their congregations were often physically out-of-doors, but they never preached to haphazard assemblies. Those to whom our Lord preached came after Him, as I feel assured crowds would in due time come after a Christian ascetic known to be settled among them. Reserve preaches much more effectually than parade of any kind.[20]

Clearly some of his anxiety here springs from the fact that he felt that large numbers of converts would be very difficult to cope with:

It may be well—possibly it is not well—to gather in converts; but a large number of converts coming in without sufficient knowledge of why they should come, would, I am sure, be more hindrance than help—a burden to look after—and at best, when the coffer comes to be opened, we should find it contained nothing but stones.[21]

When we come to consider church buildings we find Fr. Benson at his most vehement. It is clear that he was happiest worshipping in the rather temporary 'Iron Church' in Stockmore Street which he established as the centre for worship in the new parish of Cowley St. John. When we consider the passage below we have to realize that he himself built the church of St. Mary and St. John, Cowley (consecrated in 1886) and that he was writing at a time when great effort and expenditure was going into the building of new churches.

Doubtless church buildings are a necessity as the number of converts increases. But the real temple to contrast with that of Diana or Siva is the temple of the Christian community itself, the living temple, as opposed to that of stone. Surely the Community realizes its true character while it feels itself migratory and houseless. Handsome churches seem to me a necessary evil of our day where there is a Christian population and as a matter of history they have generally sprung up rather as the sepulchre than as the home of the living Church.

God gave David his wish that his son should build a glorious temple, which was of course symbolical; but how miserable was the worship of the builder, and how short-lived its glory. Then too, in Christian times, how church building reached its height of perfection just when saintliness died out. Indeed how very generally the cathedrals of Europe were built up by simple iniquity of every kind, and when built how quickly they were followed by spiritual desolation. The outward church building seems to me almost to gauge the temporal success and proportionate spiritual collapse. In a settled Christian population this is doubtless a necessity. One must endeavour to get people to erect handsome buildings because of the idea of secular glory which has so eaten into the Church's life, and which needs to be nourished like a tumour on the body; but one does feel, I think, that S. Bernard's puritan instincts were much more true, and that this outward glory is only to be tolerated as a necessity in dealing with a corrupt and worldly age of nominal Christians.[22]

Harsh words indeed, but here we see Fr. Benson's predeliction for the view of the Church as the pilgrim people of God, as we have learned it from Vatican II's *De Ecclesia*. As the Son of Man had nowhere to lay his head, so Christians must not put their trust in bricks and mortar. Grand buildings do not communicate what the gospel is about. It is interesting to see his admiration for the manner of Fr. O'Neill's life in India:

When I was shown the hovel where O'Neill lived, and the oratory where he spent hours in prayer, I could not help feeling that it was a more important place in the history of India than many a battlefield marked by crossed swords upon a map.[23]

To live in a hovel is far more glorious than worshipping in a splendid church—a truly Johannine insight!

If church buildings were an embarrassing necessity, church schools were little better. There was a real danger that people might be attracted to the faith not for the sake of the gospel but because they wanted to be educated. He did not approve of 'rice Christians'. Moreover, he was not convinced that schools in England did much more than add to the terrible number of nominal Christians. He saw it as more important to send Christians into government schools than for the Churches to run their own. He keeps on turning back to the pattern of St Paul:

One would be sorry to drop an existing school that professed Christianity, but my bias is not in favour of starting one. I think your apostolic character comes out more clearly without a school. S. Paul evidently had no thought of that kind of work. He was anxious to make the truth known to those whose hearts were touched. God drew converts to him, and God guided them as to the management of their families. . . . Schools are an element of our social superiority. We want them to accept our religion and the Christian faith upon other grounds. Social superiority has a great tendency to outshine spiritual superiority.[24]

The lower castes needed education and support for they would be the spearhead of mission in India:

The outcast tribes becoming centres of Christian life here and there throughout India will do for the future what the Jewish colonies did in the first ages, and the barbarian invasion in a later age.[25]

As we turn from these negative aspects of his views on missionary methods we may note similarities between his writings and those of Roland Allen. It is perhaps significant that while they could not be called contemporaries their lives overlapped and it could be that some of Fr. Benson's thinking influenced Allen. Certainly his first book *Missionary Methods—St. Paul's or Ours* (published in 1912) has a foreword by Fr. Waggett SSJE, which implies that some common thinking may lie behind it. Certainly Fr. Benson also looked back to the missionary methods of St. Paul and refers to them several times in his letters.

If S. Paul could have seen the Christendom which would emerge from his ministrations—well, perhaps it was as well that he did not. He probably never thought of 'this way' (Acts 9.2) becoming the way of the world as it did. So we cannot conceive of the Christianized India, which *may* come out of our missions, but indeed I hope it never will. Far better for us to think of the paradise that *certainly will* come out of them.[26]

Thus we may see that the basic pattern of missionary method which Fr. Benson is recommending is that of the 'Christian presence'. This is intimately related to his ideas about the religious life. If there are to be missionaries let them go without money, without grand buildings (he was very pleased when the Fathers moved out of the large premises at Bankipur to make room for a government medical school). Let them live the life of the cloistered Church. Let God act through them simply by their presence and their life and if they wait for years then does not this simply reflect the hidden years of the life of Christ? The most important thing was to live *in* God. The faith was not to be intellectualized; it was to be lived. Thus intercession was an essential element in mission.

More prayer and less preaching would, I believe, do more for the Church both at home and abroad. Your presence is a perpetual witness to Christ.[27]

One hears echoes of this attitude in the saying of Dietrich Bonhoeffer that 'spiritual love will speak to Christ about a brother more than to a brother about Christ'.[28]

Moreover, if there was more prayer the work of mission would be greater:

The slowness of mission work makes us realize how very little prayer is really being made by Christendom to God. If Christian people generally said 'Thy Kingdom come' as if they meant it, what consequences would there be! If we could see, we should find that God is giving far more in answer to prayer than we have a right to expect.[29]

It is by prayer, by presence, by following the pattern of Christ, that his mission is to be fulfilled. Indeed Fr. Benson would be very suspicious of the word 'success' in relation to mission. Large numbers may be given by God but they are not to be sought.

To follow Christ is to be willing to die, to give up all. Success in terms of this world may be failure in the eyes of God.

Christ came forth to meet the world and die upon the cross. They are to go forth into the same world, but they must be dead to it as he was.[30]

But this picture would give a very false impression without reference to Fr. Benson's great involvement in the establishment of parochial missions. This gained its momentum through the great Twelve Day Mission to 120 parishes in London in 1869.

This had been prepared for by a group called together by Fr. Benson and chaired by Fr. O'Neill.[31] We can trace two distinct influences behind this activity. One is the work of Robert Aiken, a Methodist lay preacher who became an Anglican vicar in Cornwall, and Richard Twigg, Tractarian vicar of St. James, Wednesbury, who both used revivalist techniques to encourage 'Catholic' churchmanship.[32]

The other seems to be the Catholic 'missions' developed by the Lazarist Fathers in eighteenth-century France.[33] These gave rise to a pattern of parish mission usually lasting ten days when the missioners through meetings and preaching and backed up by considerable prayer, sought to bring the true meaning of Catholic faith to those both inside and outside the Church. The London Mission was a major event; it was the first such mission on a large scale in this country and it set the tone for at least the next sixty years. Fr. Benson estimated that during every day of the mission there were 50,000 people present at the mission services. One interesting aspect of it was the fact that there was no theological unanimity among the clergy taking part in it and yet that did not seem to detract from its success. One outcome of this was a small handbook on *Parochial Missions* published by the Cowley Fathers to guide others in following the same pattern. The development of such missions became a major concern of the Cowley Fathers. It is difficult for us to envisage the pioneering spirit with which these missions were conducted. They were certainly used to disseminate Tractarian teaching and practice and to encourage greater commitment to Christ. Many pages of the Cowley parish magazine are full of accounts of these missions. It was another way of establishing the Christian presence in local communities.

Fr. Benson also enjoyed his parochial work. There is an interesting letter, quoted by Miss Woodgate, which shows what he thought about it:

I cannot think that parochial work is in any way injurious to the strictest religious life. The real tasks of a parish—teaching in the school, visiting the poor and sick—are rather helpful to the spiritual life and are done all the better under the restrictions of timetable. The better organized the parochial system is, the more it will fit in with monastic rule. Ministry to the children, the sick and poor has a spiritualizing effect, leading the soul to God. Indeed a hard-working curate has the advantage over us. . . . Nearness to God is not obtained by the mere absence of interruptions.[34]

Thus he was not questioning the basic structure of the Church in this way. For him neither the place nor the structure mattered very much. What mattered was to be doing the will of God and being united with him.

CHRISTIANITY AND OTHER RELIGIONS

It is hard for us to realize today how new the concept of the comparative study of religions was in Fr. Benson's time. The first major work on the subject was published by E. B. Tylor in 1871[35] and this was followed by Frazer's *Golden Bough* in 1890. We need to realize that this was a new area of thought for many people and he was keen to be involved in it. Indeed he gave a paper on comparative religion to an undergraduate society in 1875. His study of other religions led him to the conclusion that:

Other religions, even if supposed to be true, have nothing which appeals to the love of the human heart in the way that Christianity does[36]

and because God is love the gods of other religions are not gods because they are not love. He shows that he is familiar with the writings of Max Müller and chides him for putting Christianity in the same category as other religions. Hendrick Kraemer came to similar conclusions many years later.[37]

Max Müller divides religions by various differentia which he shows to be altogether valueless, and so he lets Christianity quietly down to the level of other religions. He omits one differentiating principle. Christianity is the only religion which professes to regenerate mankind, the only religion which professes to give to man the Life of God. Hinduism professes to find the Life of God in man—but man sinks lower and lower. The Life of God has ceased to profit. Christianity finds man in a state of acknowledged death and offers the gift of Life. No other religion makes the same offer.[38]

In an account of the paper he gave in 1875 he pointed out that the two main points at which Christianity was clearly differentiated from other religions were its historical and prophetical character, its dynamic character (offering life). In this way Christianity, is not so much a religion, more the divine life.

At the same time he was well aware of the deficiencies of many Christians:

Christians may well be worse than other men—according to the maxim—*corruptio optimi pessima*. The goodness of a Hindu may result from some philosophic thought personal to himself, but *not* from his *religion*. The badness of a Christian arises from his neglect of his religion, while the goodness of the very worst, as well as the saintliness of the best, springs out of the reality and power of the truth which they profess.[39]

We have already pointed out that Fr. Benson's theology of mission depends greatly on the idea of presence, the readiness of Christians to witness to Christ by living out their lives amongst people of other faiths. This presence was not to be merely inert and passive but was to be vivified by a longing for men of other faiths to find their fulfilment in Christ. This longing was very much part of his own experience during his visits to India.

I went into the Mosque which is near the Tomb, itself one of the beautiful buildings where red arches relieve the framework of the land-scape. From beneath their shade one gets another beautiful aspect of the building. Being quite by myself I was able to sing the office for None; it was a pleasure to make the arches resound with a *Gloria Patri*, as one stood where the Moulvie used to read the Koran. I dare say others have said the *Gloria* there before me, but one hopes that that glory will be hastened by many prayers, and Ishmael be called back to the tent of Isaac.[40]

But it was also true that Christians can learn from other religions. They learn first of all by comparison with the reality of Christianity. They can also see truths which need to be taken up in really indigenous Christianity. It would take time, possibly centuries, but he looks forward to the day when India would produce theologians of the calibre of the early Fathers.

There are deep religious truths mixed with the desolating falsehood of Hinduism; and as the waters leave their virtue when they dry up, so I hope Hinduism will leave a moisture behind which shall indeed be found to be the work of God's Holy Spirit, making men correspond with the kingdom of light in the life of grace. So may our ascended Lord claim India for His own, and show forth the fullness of His glory therein.[41]

THE MINISTRY

Fr. Benson was quite clear that the commission of Christ 'as my Father hath sent me, even so send I you' was not given to the ordained ministry but to the whole Church. The Holy Spirit is the unifying element—not the Bishop of Rome! There was no intention by Christ to set up a separate class of people within the Church to validate it.

The gift of the Holy Ghost was therefore a vivifying act of divine love,

by which the whole Church sprang up into the life of the Divine Sonship and the participation of the mission of Christ. It did not constitute the Apostles into a separate caste, as if the Holy Ghost dwelt with them alone. The Apostles are not a mediatorial agency separate from Christ whom they represent, or from the Church to which they minister. Christ is the personal Mediator between God and man. He acts for God towards man. He also acts for man towards God. He is both God and man. The Apostles are an agency for communicating to His members the grace of His mediation, the joints and bands by whom the nourishment is ministered to maintain the life of the whole frame. The Holy Ghost did not come to the Church through the Apostles, but He came to the Apostles and to those who were holding fellowship with them as constituting one Church, one Body, all waiting together to be quickened by His communication. Clergy and laity constitute one undivided Church, the Body of Christ.[42]

Christ is living in his Church. The historic continuity of the ministry matters because it is part of this great assertion.

The Apostles do not possess life in themselves. That is the prerogative of Christ alone, the Head. They do not transmit mechanically as conduits, but vitally as functions of the Body of Christ. The life they have from Christ is shared by all around them.[43]

Ministers are not mediators, they share the life of Christ with others. Theirs is a representative rôle in a community where all have gifts of Christ to share. But he sees this rôle as a vital one. The conditions of the Spirit's indwelling in the Church are the headship of Christ and the permanence of the apostolic ministry seen in these terms.

At the same time he sees a need for some wider diversification within the ministry. Priesthood might be expressed both in local ministries and in wider forms of mission work. He sees grave failings in the diaconate which he would like to see restored to its original function.

If only that order had been preserved in its proper integrity how much more flourishing would the Church have been. Instead of that we have nowadays very often one Priest to do pretty nearly all the work spiritual and temporal for a parish as large as the whole Church of St. Stephen's time, and then to help him there is no ordained body of almoners but a variety of committee men—not chosen because they are 'full of the Holy Ghost and wisdom' but because they have given a miserable guinea to the School or to the Missionary Society, or whatever the institution may be entrusted to their care! The spiritual life of the Priest is sacrificed to 'Charities' and by natural consequence Charity is made to be little more than a matter of money and then the physical impossibility of one man's doing it all is met by the haphazard appointment of a few men, not dedicated to this work as a sacred occupation for life, but doing it for a time because they have nothing particular to prevent their time being thus occupied. The early Christians had a very different estimate from what we have of the way in which the work of Divine Almonry should be carried out as a real but subordinate branch of the great work of Charity for which the Church was organized.[44]

Does one see in this passage reflections of the harsh realities of parochial life coming through? It certainly shows that he would have liked to have seen some wider use of the diaconate as representing another aspect of Christian discipleship.

CHRISTIAN UNITY

We have already seen in his reflections on the Virgin Birth how he sees the Church as the focal point for a new unity of the New Humanity in Christ. We must therefore see Fr. Benson as deeply committed to a wide ecumenical viewpoint. Similarly his great emphasis on the corporate nature of the Church makes him see the divisions of the Church as a scandal.

Hence we may see the grievous sacrilege which the disunion of Christendom presents. The Church does not depend for unity upon the outward union, but the powers of the unity cannot be exercised save by all acting in concert.[45]

For him the union of the Churches is broken but not the inner unity of Christ with his Church. Yet while there is division the power of the Spirit is stultified:

The action of the Holy Ghost cannot be complete in the individual unless it be complete in the Church, all the members of the undivided Apostolate being partakers of the same commission, as all the faithful also are baptised into one Spirit.[46]

Fr. Benson would not have taken easily to Church Union schemes but he was strongly committed to prayer for unity. Indeed it is as we unite in prayer that unity will come as we are all conformed to the Spirit of God:

We cannot help disunion which existed before we became Christians. We cannot continue Christians if we accept disunion, much less if we glory

in it . . . We must pray then for the Body of Christ to be manifested in its
real unity by the unitedness in thought, word and deed of all who belong
to it.[47]

His attitude to the Roman Catholic Church was very critical, his
approach to Dissenters gentle but detached. He was opposed to
controversy and preferred a gentle loving approach to others. He
saw the Church of England as being truly faithful to the will of
God, and yet he also saw that much was being lost by division.
Just because of division the action of the Church is feeble. Only as
we all drink more fully of the Spirit of God will the Church be
renewed and revitalized. Underneath all these issues lies his
main concern. The search for unity is effective insofar as it is a
search for a truly authentic expression of the gospel.

CONCLUSION

It is evident that here is no systematic theology. There are many
outward contradictions and inconsistencies in Fr. Benson's views
and they are all the more human and authentic for that. We have
seen that there lies hidden here many clues which speak more to
our age than they did to his own. There is also an inner consistency of theology which is concerned with the quality of the life of
the Church, as it represents Christ in all nations and all nations in
Christ. This quality does not come by human effort but by the
power of the procession of the Holy Spirit through the world. It
shows itself in the willingness of the Church to be despised,
rejected and persecuted in Christ's name. If that is the test of
true authenticity then the Church of our age is in many places very
authentic; for there has hardly been an age like ours for the
persecution of Christians. The Church must not adopt the
methods and standard of the age but those of Christ himself:

St. Paul . . . wanted to gather some few out of the world into Christ, not
to adapt Christ, so that all the world might accept Him. We desire to make
congregations. St. Paul desired rather to make martyrs.[48]

The Church must be shot through with mission for it lies at the
heart of God himself. Such a Church will never be still; it will be
on the move. It will be looking to the future—to the time when
that missionary spirit will be seen in all the Church.

We must pray for a missionary spirit to take hold of the whole Church. When we speak of the Church being Apostolic, we are not merely asserting the fact of the Apostolic succession, but the continuance of the Apostolical trust. If we spring from Apostles, then also Apostles must spring from us. That note of the Church has respect to the future as well as to the past. An Apostolical Church cannot be a sit-still Church.[49]

8

The Significance of Father Benson's Spirituality for Today

M. L. Smith SSJE

Thank God our time is now when wrong
Comes up to face us everywhere,
Never to leave us till we take
The longest stride of soul men ever took.
Affairs are now soul size.
The enterprise
Is exploration into God.
                 (Christopher Fry, *A Sleep of Prisoners*).

EVERY generation has to undertake its own 'exploration into God', engaging with the new demands of its own time without nostalgia or regression. There is to be no regret that 'our time is now'—an age of world-conflict when 'wrong comes up to face us everywhere', a time when the structures of societies and nations are yielding to unprecedented pressures of change and disintegration and when there is no evading the seriousness of the conflicts which rend mankind or the immensity of the forces which threaten its existence. We pursue our exploration into God guided and stimulated by our predecessors, but the nature of our time means that not all of them can be heard speaking of our condition; little help can come from those who were completely identified with the settled spirituality of a Church which had been integrated into the old social order, the Christendom now irrevocably passing away; almost none from the representatives of any merely interior and private piety. Instead from the tradition, as living participants in our struggle, there emerge more radical voices to meet our need.

    Fr. Benson was regarded in his own day within the Church of England as a man of God of almost legendary stature and after his death there continued to be a small number of followers who recognized his prophetic character and came under the influence and judgement of his teaching, teaching whose relevance was intensified by the dark forces unleashed in the first World War. Fr. Geoffrey Curtis CR speaks of his writings in this period rendering 'to his disciples the shock and stimulus that others were to gain from Kierkegaard, Karl Barth and P. T. Forsyth'.[1] The writers of these essays belong to three generations and this is a testimony to an unbroken thread of influence. But there is something especially significant in the fact that two of the longer contributions have been written by writers in their early thirties. If, as we believe, the subject of this book is of very considerable stature, it may well be that it is only as we get further away from him that we shall see the full scope and bearing of his teaching. The outline of a great mountain is best seen from a certain distance.

In claiming that the time is ripe for exploring the significance of Fr. Benson's life and thought as this modest volume of essays tries to do we are not under the illusion that he could easily or at once become a 'popular' figure. He is bound to remain uncompromisingly himself, very much on the other side of the chasm formed by a revolution in biblical interpretation and theological method, and silent about many of the issues of most passionate interest to contemporary Christians. But we do believe that those who undertake the exploration of his work will be deeply rewarded and stimulated by a spirituality so rigorous, intense and visionary.

What are some of the chief characteristics of the spirituality forged by this Victorian man of God which mark it as especially worth our deep attention? First it is a spirituality which, far from regretting, positively embraced the passing away of Christendom which he prophesied and we are experiencing. Our time has seen again martyrdom on a massive scale; confessing churches vulnerable and unprotected by assimilation to the state and society; the rapid shrinkage of religious belief and practice in the west and the breakdown of an old order in which the establishment of Christianity was maintained at the expense of its prophetic independence and of the integrity of its gospel of freedom from the conformity demanded by 'the world'. We also find young churches in what is called the third world beginning to give back to our compromised European Christianity a fresh witness to the radicalism of the gospel, and new theological insights stemming from the interaction of the faith with indigenous cultures. All these things he foresaw. In the light of these developments his writings come into their own, a crucial corrective to many pre-vailing 'liberal' voices, as a gospel for confessors conscious of the need for total conversion and of the radical discontinuity between life nourished from experience of the living God and that of 'the world'.

Secondly he taught from his own experience and in the monas-tic tradition that spiritual life involved a costly engagement with the Satanic; that there was no exploration into God which bypassed encounter with evil not as a mere external hostile influence but as a power within the soul. Prayer exposes a man to the deepest forces at work in the universe, and contemplation is the work *par excellence* which subverts the evil parasitic in crea-tion. The theme of spiritual warfare which he expounded with such power is not merely a symptom of his own coping with irrepressible energies in himself nor just an inevitable element in the ascetic tradition. It speaks to our own condition in which we have to grasp the fact that 'the line separating the good from the bad runs across the heart of every man' (Solzhenitsyn) and that demonic evil cannot be planned or persuaded away; it must be grappled with at the frontier in our own depths. Maybe in his own day Benson's concern with Satan and the figure of the Antichrist made no particular impression; it is only too relevant to a genera-tion which has seen cataclysms of warfare and undreamt of miseries. And in its light we see the dismal superficiality of those who continue with the assumption that the mystical and the prophetic are polar opposites. We see too the illusory nature of those panaceas for the world's ills offered by meditation move-ments which wholly bypass this conflict.

Then we look to him as the founder of a community. He was one of the key figures in the re-emergence of community life in the Church of England after it had for centuries been presumed defunct for ever. Now after another hundred years we see religious communities emerging in continental Protestantism under the same pressure of inspiration. It seems—the enormous influence of the Taizé community makes it difficult to deny—that there is something in the Church's very nature that demands to find expression in these communities. In the present climate of concern for community which is fostering a great variety of experiments in common life we can see that communities are infinitely more than effective religious institutions; they are of the utmost theological and spiritual significance as pointers to the true nature of the common life of the Body of Christ and expressions of the divine life itself. 'It is the law under which the Christian Church, the Body of Christ is constituted. "They had all things in common." Property belongs to the dead world. Community is the life of God.'[2]

One of the most important of Fr. Benson's insights was to see how vital it is for a religious community, while being true to its own specific style of life, to be part of a larger and more embracing unity, the Catholic Church. The tendency towards the creation of élite groups and new sects, which is endemic in all forms of fervent religion and has marked much of the history of Protestantism, can only be avoided where the genuine tension between the different callings within the Church, for instance between marriage and celibacy, between the use of property and its renunciation, is maintained and understood.

Contemporary religious communities are searching for styles of life truly appropriate to the last quarter of the twentieth century and they will be very different from that first envisaged in the 1860's for the young Society of St. John the Evangelist. But a great deal depends on whether communities today, as they shake off many of the constraints inherited from the past, can rise up to the theological vision of the religious life which inspired Fr. Benson. And though because of the idiom of his speech his thought will not be easily accessible to all, there is one particular theme in his life and writings which is of undiminished importance—the living interdependence of prayer and action. It is one of the key rôles of the saints to fuse into unity in their lives things generally supposed to be incompatible; and the popular mind supposes that there are mystics on the one hand and men of action caught up in mission and service on the other. That Fr. Benson was fully and completely both these things is no mere result of a special temperament; nor was the fact that he founded a community which was both a Society of Mission Priests and Brothers and at the same time a community with a definite contemplative and monastic orientation the result of supposing that something called 'the mixed life' provides a golden mean suitable to Anglican inclinations. Both are aspects of a single experience of

God. Since contemplation is a participation in the 'exhaustless energy' of the living God, an energy of self-communicative love, the life of prayer inevitably overflows in ministry. Equally no ministry has lasting results and no evangelism is effective which is not energized and purified by prayer. The false dichotomy between prayer and action which manifests itself today in the cultivation by some of individual spiritual experience turned in on itself, and in others by hectic activism and largely secularized styles of ministering, is a fatal weakness in much contemporary religion. The constant repetition of words which have become meaningless because they have been severed from their roots in silence and mystery is unfortunately familiar to us all. To maintain prayer and action in tension and reciprocal fruitfulness is tremendously difficult. Religious communities have it as one of their greatest tasks to do just this and to help others in different situations to do it too. Those who grasp this challenge will find much inspiration in the thought and life of Fr. Benson.

This leads us to another way in which he was a witness to the unity of things imagined to be separate; he is one of those figures who prove and anticipate the unity of the Church by showing how its separated traditions belong together and need each other. He never ceased to be an evangelical with his intense life's devotion to the scriptures, his concern for mission, personal conversion and total dedication to the person of Jesus. But it was an evangelicalism which came to its true fruition by being rooted in the early Fathers and fused with an intense sacramental Catholicism.

He wrote in one place 'By intellectual study we must gather up the teachings of the past ages in the fulness of its scope. We have not to maintain truth, but to live in the truth so that it may maintain us.'[3] This became true in himself. His insistence that the cross and resurrection need always to be seen together, his stress on the present power and action of the Holy Spirit in the Church, his sense that theology is not a matter of intellectual speculation but of living experience, corporate and personal—all these things brought him very close to the theology of the eastern Fathers and of the earlier monastic centuries in the West. As he himself recognized, something of crucial importance happened in the period of high scholasticism when theology and mysticism began to fall apart and become separate. His whole life bears witness that they are indissoluble. Without in any way ceasing to be a man of his own time, marked by its limitations as well as by its excellencies, he became a man in whom the earlier tradition came to life, became contemporary. It is striking that though he had almost no direct contact with the eastern Orthodox his instinct for the Fathers and his critical stance towards many western tendencies in spirituality and theology make him a man remarkably close to the spirit of eastern Orthodoxy. In all this there is no trace of uneasy syncretism or dilettantism; he was living the vocation of Anglicanism. He was an Anglican man of God; his life and beliefs tell us that Anglicanism is called to embody a spiritual and theological way which is not a confused and bourgeois *via media* but a demanding vocation of reconciling and living to the full evangelical and catholic faith in the spirit of the undivided Church.

Finally and most simply he is important to us because he embodies for us a precious disclosure of God. In the earthen vessels of the stern-looking books and below the rather forbidding surface of a life lived with such rigour there is the treasure of an intense love and knowledge of the living God. Our own generation has its thousands thirsty for the divine, for the contemplation and experience of God. Sources are found to satisfy this longing partially in the faiths of the East, partially in various traditions of spiritual wisdom and in esoteric cults. There is one truly inexhaustible source to which even in the Church few voices call us—the great Christian doctrines centering on the mysteries of the Trinity and Incarnation. To listen to the voice of Fr. Benson is to be summoned to approach exploration into God with a passion for truth and to assimilate these doctrinal mysteries as enabling images of incalculable power and richness which can admit us to the very life of God.

Principal Works of R. M. Benson and other Sources

Lays of Memory Sacred and Social: by a Mother and Son, London, Hurst and Blackett, 1856.

The Wisdom of the Son of David: an Exposition of the first nine Chapters of the Book of Proverbs, London, Hayes, 1860.

Redemption, London, Hayes, 1861.

Manual of Intercessory Prayer, London, Bell and Daldy, 1862.

The Divine Rule of Prayer, London, Bell and Daldy, 1866.

Bible Teachings, The Discourse at Capernaum, St. John VI, London, Hayes, 1875.

Benedictus Dominus: A course of Meditations for every day of the year, 2 vols., London, Hayes, 1879.

Spiritual Readings for Every Day:
1. Advent, London, Hayes, 1879.
2. Christmas, London, Hayes, 1880.
3. The Manifestation of Christ (Epiphany), London, Hayes, 1882.

The Final Passover: A Series of Meditations upon the Passion of our Lord Jesus Christ.

Vol. I   The Rejection, London, Hayes, 1884.

Vol. II   The Upper Chamber, Pt. 1, London, Longmans, 1895; Pt. 2, London, Longmans, 1895.

Vol. III   The Divine Exodus, Pt. 1, London, Longmans, 1893; Pt. 2, London, Longmans, 1893.

Life Beyond the Grave: A Series of Meditations upon the Resurrection and Ascension of Our Lord Jesus Christ, London, Hayes, 1885 (later published by Longmans as Vol. IV of *The Final Passover*).

The Magnificat: a Series of Meditations upon the Song of the Blessed Virgin Mary, London, Hayes, 1889.

The Virgin Birth of Our Lord, the Foundation of the Christian Religion, reprinted from *The Church Eclectic*, Boston, USA, 1894.

An Exposition of the Epistle of St. Paul to the Romans, London, J. Masters & Co., 1892.

The Followers of the Lamb: a series of Meditations especially intended for persons living under Religious Vows, and for seasons of Retreat etc., London, Longmans, 1900.

The Way of Holiness: an Exposition of Psalm 119, Analytical and Devotional, London, Methuen, 1901.

Saint Columba: a Poem, Edinburgh, St. Giles Printing Co., 1901.

The War Songs of the Prince of Peace: a Devotional Commentary on the Psalter, London, John Murray, 1901.
  Vol. 1   Helps for using the Psalter.
  Vol. 2   A Translation of the Psalter, metrical and literal, with explanatory notes and hints for spiritual instruction.
Letters of Richard Meux Benson: selected and arranged by G. Congreve and W. H. Longridge, London, Mowbray, 1916.
Further Letters of Richard Meux Benson: edited by W. H. Longridge, London, Mowbray, 1920.
Spiritual Letters of Richard Meux Benson: edited by W. H. Longridge, London, Mowbray, 1924.
Instructions on the Religious Life:
  First Series, Oxford, Society of St. John the Evangelist, 1927.
  Second Series, London, Mowbray, 1935.
  Third Series, London, Mowbray, 1951.
The Religious Vocation: edited by the Revd H. P. Bull SSJE, with an introduction by the Revd Lucius Cary SSJE, London, Mowbray, 1939.
Look to the Glory: an anthology taken from the writings and from notes made at retreats of the Reverend Richard Meux Benson compiled by the Reverend Granville Mercer Williams SSJE, Society of St. John the Evangelist Brace-bridge, Ontario, Canada, 1966.

Other Sources:
Cowley Parish Magazine, 1867–90.
Cowley Evangelist, 1891–1968.
Cowley, 1928–1974 (Cambridge, Mass., USA)
Unpublished Papers in the possession of the Society of St. John the Evangelist, Oxford.
M. V. Woodgate, *Father Benson: Founder of the Cowley Fathers*, London, Bles, 1953.

Acknowledgement:
The quotation from Christopher Fry on p.137 is reproduced from *A Sleep of Prisoners* by permission of Oxford University Press.

Notes

CHAPTER 1

1. R. W. Church, *The Oxford Movement*, Macmillan, 1891, p.139.
2. See the sermon of Pusey 'Blessed are the meek', preached at the opening of Keble College Chapel, 1874.
3. Owen Chadwick, *The Mind of the Oxford Movement*, Black, 1960, pp.48f.
4. Louis Bouyer, *Newman*, 1953, pp.223f. (Eng. trans. by J. L. May, 1958).
5. In a note to his poem for the 1st Sunday after Epiphany in *Lyra Innocentium*. See my essay on 'The Theological Vision of the Oxford Movement', in *The Rediscovery of Newman*, ed. John Coulson and A. M. Allchin, Sheed and Ward/SPCK, 1967, p.55.
6. See A. M. Allchin, *The Silent Rebellion*, SCM, 1958, chap. 11 and Woodgate, *Father Benson*, chap.5.
7. Rev. S. Gopal quoted in *Further Letters of RMB*, p.xi.
8. G. Congreve, *Christian Progress*, Longmans, 1911, p.145.
9. See C. C. J. Webb, *Religious Thought in the Oxford Movement*, SPCK, 1928, pp.90–2.
10. *Cowley Sermons*, Mowbray, 1947, pp.147–9.
11. Ibid., pp.191f.
12. *Letters of RMB*, pp.365f.
13. Ibid., pp.361–3.
14. Ibid., p.357.
15. Ibid., p.346.
16. SSJE MS.
17. SSJE MS.
18. SSJE MS.
19. V. Lossky, *The Mystical Theology of the Eastern Church*, Clarke, 1957, p.39.
20. *Followers of the Lamb*, pp.10f.
21. *Final Passover* iv, 545f.
22. The words are R. W. Church's, describing that in the Church of England which was intolerable to Newman. See R. W. Church, *Occasional Papers*, Macmillan, 1897, ii, 472.
23. Walter Lowrie, *Kierkegaard*, Harper, 1962 edn, ii, 542.
24. SSJE MS. vii, 22.
25. Lowrie, p.540.
26. Ibid.
27. Woodgate, p.155.

CHAPTER 2

1. *Chapters on Prayer*, 60.
2. *Followers of the Lamb*, p.63.
3. *Final Passover* ii, pt.2, p.330.
4. Ibid., p.322.
5. *Spiritual Letters*, p.xv.

6. *Letters of RMB*, p.187.
7. *Further Letters of RMB*, pp.235f.
8. *Letters of RMB*, p.144.
9. SSJE MS. i, 323.
10. *Further Letters of RMB*, p.89.
11. *Final Passover* ii, pt.1, pp.381f.
12. SSJE MS. vii, 144.
13. R. D. Williams, *The Theology of V. N. Lossky, an Exposition and Critique* (Bodleian Library MS. D.Phil. c.1680), p.84.
14. *Final Passover* ii, pt.2, p.370.
15. *Spiritual Readings: Advent*, p.90.
16. Williams, pp.168f.
17. *Final Passover* ii, pt. 2, p.142.
18. Ibid. p.142.
19. SSJE MS. vii, 154.
20. *Cowley Evangelist*, 1919, p.224.
21. *Religious Vocation*, p.40.
22. *Virgin Birth*, p.24.
23. *Spiritual Readings: Epiphany*, p.63.
24. From a tape quoted by Williams.
25. SSJE MS. vii, 120.
26. *Spiritual Readings: Epiphany*, pp.232, 231.
27. *Virgin Birth*, pp.35f.
28. *Further Letters of RMB*, p.297.
29. SSJE MS. vii, 156.
30. *Look to the Glory*, p.34.
31. *Cowley Evangelist*, 1919, p.145.
32. *Final Passover* ii, pt.1, p.284.
33. *Virgin Birth*, p.32.
34. *Final Passover* ii, pt.2, p.491 (my italics).
35. *Final Passover* iii, pt.2, p.374.
36. *Cowley Evangelist*, 1920, p.107.
37. *Final Passover* iii, pt.1, p.17.
38. *Final Passover* iii, pt.2, p.352.
39. Ibid., p.352.
40. *Romans*, pp.16f.
41. *Final Passover* iv, vi.
42. Ibid., p.431.
43. *Final Passover* ii, pt.2, p.450.
44. *Further Letters of RMB*, pp.268f.
45. *Final Passover* ii, pt.2, pp.205f.
46. *Church Quarterly Review*, July 1950, p.221.
47. *Final Passover* ii, pt.2, p.196.
48. Ibid., p.195.
49. *Final Passover* iv, 651.
50. *Cowley Evangelist*, 1919, pp.185f.
51. Ibid., p.205.
52. *Cowley Evangelist*, 1920, p.7.

53. *Spiritual Readings: Epiphany*, p.255.
54. *Spiritual Readings: Christmas*, p.239.
55. *Religious Vocation*, p.169.
56. *Cowley Evangelist*, 1920, p.87.
57. *Instructions*: 2nd series, p.40.
58. *Cowley Evangelist*, 1920, pp.90f.
59. *Final Passover* ii, pt.2, p.307
60. Ibid., p.312.
61. *Instructions*: 2nd series, p.44.
62. Ibid., p.68.
63. *Spiritual Readings: Christmas*, p.97.
64. Ibid., p.95.
65. *Final Passover* ii, pt.2, pp.186, 110.
66. *Final Passover* iii, pt.2, p.41.
67. *Further Letters of RMB*, pp.236f.
68. *Final Passover* i, p.403.
69. *Final Passover* ii, pt. 2, p.235.
70. Ibid., p.532.
71. *Spiritual Readings: Advent*, pp.130, 134.
72. Ibid., p.238.
73. *Further Letters of RMB*, p.129.
74. *Final Passover* ii, pt.2, p.457.
75. *Final Passover* i, p.358.
76. *Further Letters of RMB*, p.128.
77. Ibid., p.139.
78. *Cowley Evangelist*, 1920, pp.201f.
79. Ibid., p.205.
80. *Final Passover* ii, pt.1, p.397.
81. *Redemption*, p.412.

CHAPTER 3
1. *Letters of RMB*, p.204.
2. *Redemption*, pp.5, 3.
3. Ibid., p.16.
4. Ibid., p.114.
5. Ibid., p.118.
6. Ibid., pp.209f.
7. *Church Eclectic*, June 1896, p.193.
8. *Church Eclectic*, February 1897, p.967.
9. *Church Eclectic*, June 1896, p.199.
10. *Church Eclectic*, April 1897, pp.55, 53.

CHAPTER 4
1. *Further Letters*, p.288.
2. *Cowley* iii, no.9, p.9.
3. Augustine, *Confessions*, ix, 10.
4. *Lays of Memory*, p.148.
5. E. B. Pusey, *The Rationalist Character lately predominant in the Theology of*

Germany, Rivington, 1828, i, 31 (my italics).
6. H. P. Liddon, *E. B. Pusey*, Longmans, 1894, i, 152.
7. Ibid., ii, 103; iii, 105–7.
8. G. L. Prestige, *Pusey*, Philip Allan, 1933, p.123.
9. *Letters of RMB*, p.283.
10. *Further Letters of RMB*, p.11.
11. Ibid., p.25.
12. Ibid., p.137.
13. *Religious Vocation*, p.165.
14. *Followers of the Lamb*, pp.12f.
15. *Letters of RMB*, p.98.
16. 1884 MS. *SSJE Rule*, xxxii.
17. SSJE MS. xiii, 363f.
18. *Letters of RMB*, p.316 (his italics).
19. Ibid., p.310.
20. Ibid., p.325.
21. *Further Letters of RMB*, p.238.
22. *Religious Vocation*, p.276.
23. Ibid., p.190.
24. *Benedictus Dominus*, p.viii.
25. *Letters of RMB*, p.346.
26. *Further Letters of RMB*, pp.306f.
27. Woodgate, *Father Benson*, p.166.
28. B. Griffiths, *Christian Ashram*, DLT, 1966, p.43.
29. *Further Letters of RMB*, p.11.
30. SSJE MS. unpublished letter.
31. SSJE MS. unpublished letter.
32. *Letters of RMB*, p.334.
33. *Wisdom of the Son of David*, p.xi (my italics).
34. *War Songs of the Prince of Peace*, i, 41.
35. Ambrose, *Hom. xiii in Nat. Dom.*
36. G. W. H. Lampe and K. J. Woollcombe, *Essays on Typology*, SCM, 1957, p.31.
37. *War Songs*, i, 5.
38. Ibid., p.8.
39. Ibid., p.13.
40. Ibid., ii, 3.
41. Ibid., i, 10.
42. Ibid., ii, 221.
43. *Religious Vocation*, pp.183f.
44. Ibid., pp.170f.
45. *War Songs*, i, 31.
46. T. Merton, *On the Psalms*, Sheldon, 1977, p.13.
47. SSJE MS. unpublished letter (my italics).
48. D. Bonhoeffer, *Life Together*, SCM, 1963, p.36.
49. E. Bethge, *Dietrich Bonhoeffer*, Collins, 1970, p.105.
50. *Followers of the Lamb*, p.11.
51. Ibid., p.12.
52. G. L. Prestige, *Life of Charles Gore*, Heinemann, 1935, p.105.

53. Woodgate, p.152.
54. *Letters of RMB*, p.115.
55. Ibid., pp.327f.
56. *Instructions*, 3rd series, p.88.

CHAPTER 5
1. *Cowley Evangelist*, 1920, p.32.
2. *Cowley Evangelist*, 1924, pp.198f.
3. *Letters of RMB*, p.358.
4. *The Glass of Vision*, Dacre, 1948, p.43.
5. Ibid., p.44.
6. Ibid., p.49.
7. *Letters of RMB*, pp. 155f.
8. *Further Letters of RMB*, p.44.
9. *Religious Vocation*, p.157.
10. *Letters of RMB*, pp.320f.
11. *Further Letters of RMB*, p.299.
12. Ibid., p.188.
13. *Religious Vocation*, p.95.
14. Ibid., p.49.
15. SSJE MS. xii, 532.
16. *Religious Vocation*, p.86.
17. SSJE MS. iv, 217.
18. Ibid., p.224.
19. Ibid., p.244.
20. *Cowley Evangelist*, 1918, p.29.
21. *Cowley Evangelist*, 1920, pp.4f.
22. Ibid., p.7.
23. Ibid., p.8.
24. *Spiritual Readings: Christmas*, p.49.
25. Ibid., pp.33f.
26. *Cowley Evangelist*, 1920, p.46.
27. *Followers of the Lamb*, p.113.
28. *Further Letters of RMB*, p.279.
29. *Letters of RMB*, pp.246f.
30. *Cowley Evangelist*, 1920, p.86.
31. *Benedictus Dominus*, p.ix.
32. *Spiritual Readings: Christmas*, p.48.
33. *Religious Vocation*, pp.200f.
34. Ibid., p.190.
35. *Further Letters of RMB*, p.315.
36. Ibid., pp.316f.
37. Ibid., p.251.
38. *Letters of RMB*, p.107.
39. *Further Letters of RMB*, pp.46f.
40. *Manual of Intercessory Prayer*, pp.41f.
41. *Final Passover* ii, pt. 2, p.307.
42. *Instructions*, 3rd series, p.109.

43. Ibid., p.111.
44. Ibid., p.108.
45. *A Celebration of Faith*, Hodder, 1970, pp.164f.
46. SSJE MS. i, 547.
47. *Instructions*, 3rd series, pp.87f.
48. *Further Letters of RMB*, p.139.
49. *Followers of the Lamb*, p.6.
50. Ibid., p.103.
51. Ibid. p.5.
52. *Further letters of RMB*, p.299.
53. Ibid., pp.299, 300.
54. Ibid., p.59.
55. Ibid., p.43.
56. Ibid., p.93.
57. *Cowley Evangelist*, 1924, p.196.
58. *Instructions*, 3rd series, p.11.
59. *Instructions*, 2nd series, pp.36f.
60. Ibid., p.82.
61. *Cowley*, iii, no.9, p.11.
62. *Treasures of Hope for the Evening of Life*, Longmans, 1918, p.189. Fr. Congreve relates how a lady whom Fr. Benson visited in her last illness showed him Hugo's poem which he there and then rendered into the version here quoted. The original words are:
> Soyons comme l'oiseau
> Posé pour un instant
> Sur des rameaux trop frêles,
>   Qui sent trembler la branche,
> Mais chante pourtant,
> Sachant qu'il a des ailes.

CHAPTER 6
1. *Instructions*, 2nd series, p.34.
2. *Letters of RMB*, p.298.
3. Ibid., p.266.
4. Ibid., p.255.
5. Ibid., p.171.
6. *Followers of the Lamb*, p.6.
7. G. Congreve, *Christian Progress*, Longmans, 1911, p.vi.
8. *Final Passover* iv, 278.
9. Ibid., p.289.
10. SSJE MS. vii, 22.
11. *Commentary on the Canticle* 1029a–1037c, trans. H. Musurillo in *From Glory to Glory*, John Murray, 1962.
12. *Instructions*, 2nd series, p.69.
13. J. G. Lockhart, *Viscount Halifax*, Geoffrey Bles, 1935, i, 83f.
14. E. C. Hoskyns, *The Fourth Gospel*, Faber, 1941, p.41.
15. *Religious Vocation*, p.272.
16. SSJE MS. vii, 136.

17. SSJE MS. vi, Ret. of 1873.
18. *Letters of RMB*, p.229.
19. Ibid., pp.233f.
20. G. Congreve, *Christian Progress*, p.204.
21. *SSJE Rule*, vii, 'Of Profession'.
22. Milton, *Paradise Lost*, x, 783.
23. SSJE MS. vii. 138.
24. *SSJE Rule*, vii, 'Of the Cell'.
25. *Final Passover* iv, 400.
26. Ibid., p.417.
27. Ibid., p.423.
28. Ibid., p.422.
29. Ibid., p.476.
30. Ibid., p.426.
31. *Cowley Evangelist*, 1918, p.75.
32. *Instructions*, 2nd series, p.19.
33. Ibid., p.21.
34. *Letters of RMB*, p.372.
35. Ibid., pp.59f.
36. Ibid., p.139.
37. Ibid., p.183.
38. *Cowley Evangelist*, 1918, p.53.
39. *SSJE Rule*, ix, 'Of Poverty'.
40. *Instructions*, 2nd series, p.21.
41. *Instructions*, 3rd series, p.13.
42. *Followers of the Lamb*, p.6.
43. *Letters of RMB*, p.299.

CHAPTER 7
1. *Further Letters of RMB*, p.165.
2. *Letters of RMB*, p.326.
3. *Final Passover* ii, pt.2, p.108.
4. Ibid., p.109.
5. *Further Letters*, p.161.
6. *Virgin Birth*, p.35.
7. Ibid., p.36.
8. Ibid., p.37.
9. Ibid., p.38.
10. Ibid., p.38.
11. See for instance, the WCC Report *The Church for Others*, which lays great emphasis on the fact that we do not have a mission but share in the mission of Christ.
12. *Final Passover* iv, 495.
13. *Final Passover* iii, pt.2, p.30.
14. *Further Letters of RMB*, p.295.
15. *Final Passover* i, ix.
16. *Followers of the Lamb*, p.3.
17. *Final Passover* iv, 404.

18. *Final Passover* iii, pt.2, pp.263, 265.
19. *Further Letters of RMB*, p.223.
20. *Letters of RMB*, p.160.
21. Ibid., p.165.
22. *Further Letters of RMB*, pp.225f.
23. Woodgate, *Father Benson*, p.155.
24. *Further Letters of RMB*, p.95.
25. Ibid., p.125.
26. Ibid., p.62.
27. Ibid., p.231.
28. *Life Together*, SCM, 1954, p.26. An interesting parallel between the thinking of Benson and Bonhoeffer can be made at many points. Both were fascinated by India, both very much concerned with community and the hidden life. It is by no means irrelevant that Bonhoeffer spent some time at the Mission House in 1934.
29. *Further Letters of RMB*, p.42.
30. *Final Passover* ii, pt. 2, p.482.
31. A brief account is given in *Catholic Evangelicalism* by Dieter Voll, Faith Press, 1963, p.49, and there is a chapter in *Memoir of George Howard Wilkinson* by A. J. Mason, Longmans, 1909, i, 227ff. See also *Cowley S. John Parish Mag.*, Dec. 1869.
32. See D. Voll op. cit.
33. See John Kent, *Holding the Fort*, Epworth Press, 1978. This book gives details of the influence of the French Missions and also contains a chapter on 'Anglo-Catholic Revivalism' which describes the 1869 Mission to London.
34. Woodgate, p.144.
35. Tylor was the first Professor of Anthropology at Oxford (1884–9 as Reader, 1896–1909 as Professor); Benson may have known him.
36. *Letters of RMB*, p.40.
37. See his *Christian Message in a Non-Christian World*, Edinburgh House Press, 1937.
38. *Letters of RMB*, p.41.
39. Ibid., p.42.
40. Ibid., p.63.
41. *Further Letters of RMB*, p.190.
42. *Final Passover* iv, 504f.
43. Ibid., p.505.
44. *Cowley S. John Parish Mag.*, Sept. 1869.
45. *Final Passover* ii, pt. 2, p.481.
46. Ibid., p.482.
47. *Cowley S. John Parish Mag.*, Sept. 1872.
48. *Romans*, p.483.
49. *Cowley S. John Parish Mag.*, Dec. 1872.

CHAPTER 8

1. *Church Quarterly Review*, Sept. 1950, p.218.
2. SSJE MS. vii, 156.
3. *Followers of the Lamb*, p.13.